Second Editon

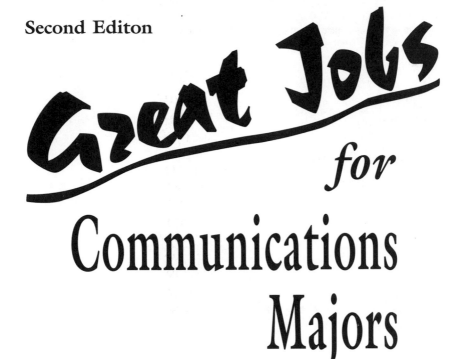

Great Jobs

for

Communications Majors

Blythe Camenson

SERIES DEVELOPERS AND CONTRIBUTING AUTHORS
Stephen E. Lambert
Julie Ann DeGalan

VGM Career Books
Chicago New York San Francisco Lisbon London Madrid Mexico City
Milan New Delhi San Juan Seoul Singapore Sydney Toronto

Library of Congress Cataloging-in-Publication Data

Camenson, Blythe.
    Great jobs for communications majors 2nd ed. / Blythe Camenson.
        p.   cm. — (Great jobs for—)
    Includes index.
    ISBN 0-658-01765-9
    1. Communication—Vocational guidance.   I. Title.   II. Series.

P91.6.C363   2001
302.2'023—dc21   2001035766

VGM Career Books

A Division of The **McGraw·Hill** *Companies*

1 2 3 4 5 6 7 8 9 0   LBM/LBM   0 9 8 7 6 5 4 3 2 1

ISBN 0-658-01765-9

This book was set in Adobe Garamond
Printed and bound by Lake Book Manufacturing

McGraw-Hill books are available at special quantity discounts to use as premiums and
sales promotions, or for use in corporate training programs. For more information, please
write to the Director of Special Sales, Professional Publishing, McGraw-Hill, Two Penn
Plaza, New York, NY 10121-2298. Or contact your local bookstore.

This book is printed on acid-free paper.

To Tom Henkel, who let me vent, and to Sarah Kennedy, who held my hand

CONTENTS

ACKNOWLEDGMENTS

Anthony Clark, Director of Undergraduate Studies, Communication Studies Program, University of Florida, Gainesville, Florida.

Mary A. Dustin, Career Counselor, Career Service Center, Cleveland State University, Cleveland, Ohio.

Marshall J. Cook, Professor, University of Wisconsin–Madison Outreach Program, Communications Department, Madison, Wisconsin.

Scott Griffiths, Graduate Coordinator, Communication Disorders, University of Florida, Gainesville, Florida.

Norman Leaper, ABC, President, International Association of Business Communicators (IABC), San Francisco, California.

Rebecca Torres, Community Relations Coordinator, Books-A-Million, Sunrise, Florida.

COMMUNICATIONS: A DEGREE WITH NO BOUNDARIES

*E*very day we are bombarded with words, messages, and information, whether oral, written, televised, faxed, phoned, or E-mailed. We are informed, persuaded, influenced, motivated, directed, led, counseled, helped, entertained, and, sometimes, annoyed by all the communication with which we are confronted.

But there's no escaping it. Whether in school, at work, or on the home front, we are constantly receiving and exchanging information. Professors strive to stimulate their students; bosses hope to keep their employees motivated and productive; our mailboxes are crammed full of notices, advertisements, and all sorts of enticements to buy or act; the telephone, television, radio, newspapers, books, and magazines all vie for our attention.

Although many Americans might resent the constant intrusion, to communications majors it's a godsend. Such an all-pervasive focus on communication and information means unlimited opportunities for finding exciting and challenging work.

THE INFORMATION INDUSTRY

The information industry outranks any other and in the past four decades has become the central nucleus of the economy and labor force of the United States.

The twentieth century saw a rapid shift through four stages. We went from an agrarian society to an industry- then service-based economy, through today, to an economy-based society and dependent on a rapid exchange of information.

In the early 1900s, agriculture made up almost 40 percent of the labor force, compared to today's figure of approximately only 5 percent. Industry continued to grow through 1960 or so, then started a decline, which has since leveled off, now claiming only about 25 percent of the workforce. As industrial activities waned, the service industry flourished.

But the information industry has bypassed them all. There are now more workers employed in some facet of the information industry than in any other sector. In fact, more than 50 percent of the country's workforce earns its living dealing with information.

COMMUNICATIONS: PAST AND PRESENT

Communciation is as old as mankind itself; communication as a tool for influencing behavior and opinion dates back to the early Greeks and Romans. This early definition of communications, as a means of persuasion, was held until only twenty years or so ago. In the sixties and seventies—even as late as the early to mid-eighties—communications was considered a degree for the media and business industry, corporate organizations, advertising, and PR.

These days, a communications degree crosses those boundaries or ignores them completely. The value of a communications degree is widely recognized as the backbone of myriad fields. In addition to the more familiar media and business applications, communications skills have now been earmarked as important in law, government, and international relations; in health and human and social services; in education; in working with speech and language disorders; in information sciences; and in arts and entertainment.

The Speech Communication Association has identified the following diverse areas of specialization typically offered in college and university communications departments:

Advertising	Journalism
Education	Legal communication
Family communication	Mass communication
Forensics, argumentation, and debate	Media and communication technologies and policy
Health communication	
Information sciences and human information systems	Organizational communication
	Political communication
Instructional development	Public relations
International and intercultural communication	Radio, television, and film
	Rhetorical and communication theory
Interpersonal and small group interaction	Speech and language sciences
	Theater
Interpretation and performance studies	

Choosing a specialization must, by necessity, be one of the first tasks facing any potential communications major. Because university programs vary so much, a student hoping to land a job with an ad agency would not be well served by a department whose main focus was on intercultural communication. Locating a suitable program will be covered more fully in Chapter 9.

THE ROLE OF THE PROFESSIONAL COMMUNICATOR

Communications serves one or more of the following four functions: to persuade, to educate, to inform, to entertain. This is generally accomplished through words, images, and sounds.

In a broad sense, professional communicators, or communication specialists, plan and devise information systems that link the industry with specific audiences. They decide what information should be transmitted and how it should be channeled, and in some cases, they research the potential impact or social consequences on a diverse culture. They might also generate new information.

Communications professionals, in addition to being versed in communications theory, must be familiar with the different techniques and technology of their chosen specialization. For example, where journalists once functioned with only manual typewriters, they now must be fully adept at word processing, and perhaps even be familiar with computer graphics and distribution technologies.

Law students, who might have earned their bachelor's degree in communications, know the importance of understanding theories of rhetorical criticism as it applies to the appraisal of spoken persuasive discourse.

Foreign service officers need an understanding of techniques for effective intercultural communication; audiologists must keep current on all the latest devices for assessing the performance of hearing aids. The list of examples seems limitless.

In discussing the role of the communications specialist, the Speech Communications Association, in their publication *Pathways to Careers in Communications*, lists four "inescapable conclusions":

1. Regardless of one's chosen occupation, the ability to manipulate information and to communicate effectively has rapidly become an essential component of every sector of the U.S. economy.

2. Virtually every individual requires training and skill as an information processor and communicator in order to exist effectively within the information society.

3. Communications specialists facilitate the transformation of information into meaningful knowledge for human beings.

4. The changing composition of the labor force and consumers in the information society requires that all individuals in all occupations understand and acquire the skills necessary to respond effectively in culturally diverse employment and market environments.

THE IDEAL COMMUNICATIONS SPECIALIST

The ideal communications specialist might, in actuality, be a generalist. Today's communications majors learn a wide range of skills, with just as wide a range of applications. But a variety of studies shows that the most important skill is still the ability to communicate effectively.

Employers, returning to the hiring patterns of two or three decades ago, are now looking for graduates with liberal arts backgrounds. They are shunning individuals with technical or job-specific training in favor of those who show themselves to be competent communicators, both in person and on paper. The results of a survey canvassing chief executive officers based in New York point to the "ability to express ideas verbally" as the most important criteria used to screen and evaluate job candidates. The survey (conducted by Silverstone, Greenbaum, and MacGregor, and presented in their unpublished paper, "The Preferred College Graduate as Seen by the NY Business Community") concluded that "they [CEOs] don't seem to want 'salesmen,' business 'intellectuals,' or 'ready-made' business executives (with an MBA in hand). They do want team-players who can express themselves with substance in ideas and thoughts."

These days, this response from the business community can be transferred to just about any field. Whether approached as a terminal degree or a steppingstone, a major in communications will open more doors than almost any other course of study.

PART ONE

THE JOB SEARCH

CHAPTER ONE

THE SELF-ASSESSMENT

elf-assessment is the process by which you begin to acknowledge your own particular blend of education, experiences, values, needs, and goals. It provides the foundation for career planning and the entire job search process. Self-assessment involves looking inward and asking yourself what can sometimes prove to be difficult questions. This self-examination should lead to an intimate understanding of your personal traits, your personal values, your consumption patterns and economic needs, your longer-term goals, your skill base, your preferred skills, and your underdeveloped skills.

You come to the self-assessment process knowing yourself well in some of these areas, but you may still be uncertain about other aspects. You may be well aware of your consumption patterns, but have you spent much time specifically identifying your longer-term goals or your personal values as they relate to work? No matter what level of self-assessment you have undertaken to date, it is now time to clarify all of these issues and questions as they relate to the job search.

The knowledge you gain in the self-assessment process will guide the rest of your job search. In this book, you will learn about all of the following tasks:

- Writing resumes

- Exploring possible job titles

- Identifying employment sites

- Networking

- Interviewing

- Following up

- Evaluating job offers

In each of these steps, you will rely on and often return to the understanding gained through your self-assessment. Any individual seeking employment must be able and willing to express these facets of his or her personality to recruiters and interviewers throughout the job search. This communication allows you to show the world who you are so that together with employers you can determine whether there will be a workable match with a given job or career path.

HOW TO CONDUCT A SELF-ASSESSMENT

The self-assessment process goes on naturally all the time. People ask you to clarify what you mean, you make a purchasing decision, or you begin a new relationship. You react to the world, and the world reacts to you. How you understand these interactions and any changes you might make because of them are part of the natural process of self-discovery. There is, however, a more comprehensive and efficient way to approach self-assessment with regard to employment.

Because self-assessment can become a complex exercise, we have distilled it into a seven-step process that provides an effective basis for undertaking a job search. The seven steps include the following:

1. Understanding your personal traits

2. Identifying your personal values

3. Calculating your economic needs

4. Exploring your longer-term goals

5. Enumerating your skill base

6. Recognizing your preferred skills

7. Assessing skills needing further development

As you work through your self-assessment, you might want to create a worksheet similar to the one shown in Exhibit 1.1 starting on the following page. Or you might want to keep a journal of the thoughts you have as you

Exhibit 1.1

SELF-ASSESSMENT WORKSHEET

STEP 1. Understand Your Personal Traits
>The personal traits that describe me are:
>*(Include all of the words that describe you.)*

>The ten personal traits that most accurately describe me are:
>*(List these ten traits.)*

STEP 2. Identify Your Personal Values
>Working conditions that are important to me include:
>*(List working conditions that would have to exist for you to accept a position.)*

>The values that go along with my working conditions are:
>*(Write down the values that correspond to each working condition.)*

>Some additional values I've decided to include are:
>*(List those values you identify as you conduct this job search.)*

STEP 3. Calculate Your Economic Needs
>My estimated minimum annual salary requirement is:
>*(Write the salary you have calculated based on your budget.)*

>Starting salaries for the positions I'm considering are:
>*(List the name of each job you are considering and the associated starting salary.)*

STEP 4. Explore Your Longer-Term Goals
>My thoughts on longer-term goals right now are:
>*(Jot down some of your longer-term goals as you know them right now.)*

STEP 5. Enumerate Your Skill Base
>The general skills I possess are:
>*(List the skills that underlie tasks you are able to complete.)*

>The specific skills I possess are:
>*(List more technical or specific skills that you possess, and indicate your level of expertise.)*

General and specific skills that I want to promote to employers for the jobs I'm considering are:
(List general and specific skills for each type of job you are considering.)

STEP 6. Recognize Your Preferred Skills
Skills that I would like to use on the job include:
(List skills that you hope to use on the job, and indicate how often you'd like to use them.)

STEP 7. Assess Skills Needing Further Development
Some skills that I'll need to acquire for the jobs I'm considering include:
(Write down skills listed in job advertisements or job descriptions that you don't currently possess.)

I believe I can build these skills by:
(Describe how you plan to acquire these skills.)

undergo this process. There will be many opportunities to revise your self-assessment as you start down the path of seeking a career.

STEP 1 Understanding Your Personal Traits

Each person has a unique personality that he or she brings to the job search process. Gaining a better understanding of your personal traits can help you evaluate job and career choices. Identifying these traits and then finding employment that allows you to draw on at least some of them can create a rewarding and fulfilling work experience. If potential employment doesn't allow you to use these preferred traits, it is important to decide whether you can find other ways to express them or whether you would be better off not considering this type of job. Interests and hobbies pursued outside of work hours can be one way to use personal traits you don't have an opportunity to draw on in your work. For example, if you consider yourself an outgoing person and the kinds of jobs you are examining allow little contact with other people, you may be able to achieve the level of interaction that is comfortable for you outside of your work setting. If such a compromise seems impractical or otherwise unsatisfactory, you probably should explore only jobs that provide the interaction you want and need on the job.

Many young adults who are not very confident about their attractiveness to employers will downplay their need for income. They will say, "Money is not all that important if I love my work." But if you begin to document exactly what you need for housing, transportation, insurance, clothing, food, and utilities, you will begin to understand that some jobs cannot meet your financial needs and it doesn't matter how wonderful the job is. If you have to worry each payday about bills and other financial obligations, you won't be very effective on the job. Begin now to be honest with yourself about your needs.

Inventorying Your Personal Traits. Begin the self-assessment process by creating an inventory of your personal traits. Using the list in Exhibit 1.2, decide which of these personal traits describe you.

Exhibit 1.2

PERSONAL TRAITS

Accurate	Considerate	Fair-minded
Active	Cool	Farsighted
Adaptable	Cooperative	Feeling
Adventurous	Courageous	Firm
Affectionate	Critical	Flexible
Aggressive	Curious	Formal
Ambitious	Daring	Friendly
Analytical	Decisive	Future-oriented
Appreciative	Deliberate	Generous
Artistic	Detail-oriented	Gentle
Brave	Determined	Good-natured
Businesslike	Discreet	Helpful
Calm	Dominant	Honest
Capable	Eager	Humorous
Caring	Easygoing	Idealistic
Cautious	Efficient	Imaginative
Cheerful	Emotional	Impersonal
Clean	Empathetic	Independent
Competent	Energetic	Individualistic
Confident	Excitable	Industrious
Conscientious	Expressive	Informal
Conservative	Extroverted	Innovative

Intellectual	Peaceable	Self-disciplined
Intelligent	Personable	Sensible
Introverted	Persuasive	Sensitive
Intuitive	Pleasant	Serious
Inventive	Poised	Sincere
Jovial	Polite	Sociable
Just	Practical	Spontaneous
Kind	Precise	Strong
Liberal	Principled	Strong-minded
Likable	Private	Structured
Logical	Productive	Subjective
Loyal	Progressive	Tactful
Mature	Quick	Thorough
Methodical	Quiet	Thoughtful
Meticulous	Rational	Tolerant
Mistrustful	Realistic	Trusting
Modest	Receptive	Trustworthy
Motivated	Reflective	Truthful
Objective	Relaxed	Understanding
Observant	Reliable	Unexcitable
Open-minded	Reserved	Uninhibited
Opportunistic	Resourceful	Verbal
Optimistic	Responsible	Versatile
Organized	Reverent	Wholesome
Original	Sedentary	Wise
Outgoing	Self-confident	
Patient	Self-controlled	

Focusing on Selected Personal Traits. Of all the traits you identified from the list in Exhibit 1.2, select the ten you believe most accurately describe you. If you are having a difficult time deciding, think about which words people who know you well would use to describe you. Keep track of these ten traits.

Considering Your Personal Traits in the Job Search Process. As you begin exploring jobs and careers, watch for matches between your personal traits and the job descriptions you read. Some jobs will require many personal traits you know you possess, and others will not seem to match those traits.

· ·

A freelance writer's work, for example, requires self-dicipline, motivation, curiosity, and observation. Authors usually work alone, with limited opportunities to interact with others. A corporate trainer, on the other hand, must interact regularly with staff or clients to carry out training programs. Corporate trouble-shooters need strong interpersonal and verbal skills, imagination, and a good sense of humor. They must enjoy being up in front of groups and must become skilled at presenting information using a variety of media.

· ·

Your ability to respond to changing conditions, your decision-making ability, productivity, creativity, and verbal skills all have a bearing on your success in and enjoyment of your work life. To better guarantee success, be sure to take the time needed to understand these traits in yourself.

STEP 2 Identifying Your Personal Values

Your personal values affect every aspect of your life, including employment, and they develop and change as you move through life. Values can be defined as principles that we hold in high regard, qualities that are important and desirable to us. Some values aren't ordinarily connected to work (love, beauty, color, light, relationships, family, or religion), and others are (autonomy, cooperation, effectiveness, achievement, knowledge, and security). Our values determine, in part, the level of satisfaction we feel in a particular job.

Defining Acceptable Working Conditions. One facet of employment is the set of working conditions that must exist for someone to consider taking a job.

Each of us would probably create a unique list of acceptable working conditions, but items that might be included on many people's lists are the amount of money you would need to be paid, how far you are willing to drive or travel, the amount of freedom you want in determining your own schedule, whether you would be working with people or data or things, and the types of tasks you would be willing to do. Your conditions might include statements of working conditions you will *not* accept; for example, you might not be willing to work at night or on weekends or holidays.

If you were offered a job tomorrow, what conditions would have to exist for you to realistically consider accepting the position? Take some time and make a list of these conditions.

Exhibit 1.3

WORK VALUES

Achievement	Development	Physical activity
Advancement	Effectiveness	Power
Adventure	Excitement	Precision
Attainment	Fast pace	Prestige
Authority	Financial gain	Privacy
Autonomy	Helping	Profit
Belonging	Humor	Recognition
Challenge	Improvisation	Risk
Change	Independence	Security
Communication	Influencing others	Self-expression
Community	Intellectual stimulation	Solitude
Competition	Interaction	Stability
Completion	Knowledge	Status
Contribution	Leading	Structure
Control	Mastery	Supervision
Cooperation	Mobility	Surroundings
Creativity	Moral fulfillment	Time freedom
Decision making	Organization	Variety

Realizing Associated Values. Your list of working conditions can be used to create an inventory of your values relating to jobs and careers you are exploring. For example, if one of your conditions stated that you wanted to earn at least $30,000 per year, the associated value would be financial gain. If another condition was that you wanted to work with a friendly group of people, the value that went along with that might be belonging or interaction with people. Exhibit 1.3 provides a list of commonly held values that relate to the work environment; use it to create your own list of personal values.

Relating Your Values to the World of Work. As you read the job descriptions in this book and in other suggested resources, think about the values associated with each position.

· ·

For example, the duties of a reporter would include researching, investigating, and conducting interviews; organizing the information in a logical format; and writ-

ing and editing articles and profiles. Associated values are
intellectual stimulation, organization, communication, and
creativity.

....

If you were thinking about a career in this field, or any other field you're
exploring, at least some of the associated values should match those you
extracted from your list of working conditions. Take a second look at any
values that don't match up. How important are they to you? What will happen if they are not satisfied on the job? Can you incorporate those personal
values elsewhere? Your answers need to be brutally honest. As you continue
your exploration, be sure to add to your list any additional values that occur
to you.

STEP 3   Calculating Your Economic Needs

Each of us grew up in an environment that provided for certain basic needs,
such as food and shelter, and, to varying degrees, other needs that we now
consider basic, such as cable television, E-mail, or an automobile. Needs such
as privacy, space, and quiet, which at first glance may not appear to be mon-
etary needs, may add to housing expenses and so should be considered as
you examine your economic needs. For example, if you place a high value
on a large, open living space for yourself, it would be difficult to satisfy that
need without an associated high housing cost, especially in a densely populated city environment.

As you prepare to move into the world of work and become responsible
for meeting your own basic needs, it is important to consider the salary you
will need to be able to afford a satisfying standard of living. The three-step
process outlined here will help you plan a budget, which in turn will allow
you to evaluate the various career choices and geographic locations you are
considering. The steps include (1) developing a realistic budget, (2) examining starting salaries, and (3) using a cost-of-living index.

Developing a Realistic Budget. Each of us has certain expectations for the
kind of lifestyle we want to maintain. To begin the process of defining your
economic needs, it will be helpful to determine what you expect to spend
on routine monthly expenses. These expenses include housing, food, transportation, entertainment, utilities, loan repayments, and revolving charge
accounts. A worksheet that details many of these expenses is shown in
Exhibit 1.4. You may not currently spend anything for certain items, but you
probably will have to once you begin supporting yourself. As you develop
this budget, be generous in your estimates, but keep in mind any items that

Exhibit 1.4

ESTIMATED MONTHLY EXPENSES WORKSHEET

		Could Reduce Spending? (Yes/No)
Cable	$ _____	_____
Child care	_____	_____
Clothing	_____	_____
Educational loan repayment	_____	_____
Entertainment	_____	_____
Food		
At home	_____	_____
Meals out	_____	_____
Gifts	_____	_____
Housing		
Rent/mortgage	_____	_____
Insurance	_____	_____
Property taxes	_____	_____
Medical insurance	_____	_____
Reading materials		
Newspapers	_____	_____
Magazines	_____	_____
Books	_____	_____
Revolving loans/charges	_____	_____
Savings	_____	_____
Telephone	_____	_____
Transportation	_____	_____
Auto payment	_____	_____
Insurance	_____	_____
Parking	_____	_____
Gasoline	_____	_____
or		
Cab/train/bus fare	_____	_____
Utilities		
Electric	_____	_____
Gas	_____	_____
Water/sewer	_____	_____
Vacations	_____	_____

		Could Reduce Spending? (Yes/No)
Miscellaneous expense 1	_____	_____
Expense: _____		
Miscellaneous expense 2	_____	_____
Expense: _____		
Miscellaneous expense 3	_____	_____
Expense: _____		

TOTAL MONTHLY EXPENSES: _____

YEARLY EXPENSES (Monthly expenses × 12): _____ _____

INCREASE TO INCLUDE TAXES (Yearly expenses × 1.35): _____ _____ =

MINIMUM ANNUAL SALARY REQUIREMENT: _____ _____

could be reduced or eliminated. If you are not sure about the cost of a certain item, talk with family or friends who would be able to give you a realistic estimate.

If this is new or difficult for you, start to keep a log of expenses right now. You may be surprised at how much you actually spend each month for food or stamps or magazines. Household expenses and personal grooming items can often loom very large in a budget, as can auto repairs or home maintenance.

Income taxes must also be taken into consideration when examining salary requirements. State and local taxes vary, so it is difficult to calculate exactly the effect of taxes on the amount of income you need to generate. To roughly estimate the gross income necessary to generate your minimum annual salary requirement, multiply the minimum salary you have calculated (see Exhibit 1.4) by a factor of 1.35. The resulting figure will be an approximation of what your gross income would need to be, given your estimated expenses.

Examining Starting Salaries. Starting salaries for each of the career tracks are provided throughout this book. These salary figures can be used in conjunction with the cost-of-living index (discussed in the next section) to determine whether you would be able to meet your basic economic needs in a given geographic location.

Using a Cost-of-Living Index. If you are thinking about trying to get a job in a geographic region other than the one where you now live, understanding differences in the cost of living will help you come to a more informed decision about making a move. By using a cost-of-living index, you can compare salaries offered and the cost of living in different locations with what you know about the salaries offered and the cost of living in your present location.

Many variables are used to calculate the cost-of-living index. Often included are housing, groceries, utilities, transportation, health care, clothing, and entertainment expenses. Right now you do not need to worry about the details associated with calculating a given index. The main purpose of this exercise is to help you understand that pay ranges for entry-level positions may not vary greatly, but the cost of living in different locations *can* vary tremendously.

. . . .

If you lived in Cleveland, Ohio, for example, and you were interested in working as a photojournalist for the *Cleveland Plain Dealer*, you would earn just over $500 per week to start ($26,643 annually). But let's say you're also thinking about moving to either New York, Los Angeles, or Minneapolis. You know you can live on $26,643 in Cleveland, but you want to be able to equal that salary in the other locations you're considering. How much will you have to earn in those locations to do this? Figuring the cost of living for each city will show you.

Let's walk through this example. In any cost-of-living index, the number 100 represents the national average cost of living, and each city is assigned an index number based on current prices in that city for the items included in the index (housing, food, and so forth). In the index we used, New York was assigned the number 213.3, Los Angeles was assigned 124.6, Minneapolis was assigned 104.6, and the index for Cleveland was 114.3. In other words, it costs almost twice as much to live in New York as it does in Cleveland. We can set up a table to determine exactly how much you would have to earn in each of these cities to have the same buying power that you have in Cleveland.

JOB: PHOTOJOURNALIST

City	Index	Equivalent Salary

$$\frac{\text{New York} \quad 213.3}{\text{Cleveland} \quad 114.3} \times \$26{,}643 = \$49{,}720 \text{ in New York}$$

$$\frac{\text{Los Angeles} \quad 124.6}{\text{Cleveland} \quad 114.3} \times \$26{,}643 = \$29{,}044 \text{ in Los Angeles}$$

$$\frac{\text{Minneapolis} \quad 104.6}{\text{Cleveland} \quad 114.3} \times \$26{,}643 = \$24{,}382 \text{ in Minneapolis}$$

You would have to earn $49,720 in New York, $29,044 in Los Angeles, and $24,382 in Minneapolis to match the buying power of $26,643 in Cleveland.

If you would like to determine whether it's financially worthwhile to make any of these moves, one more piece of information is needed: the salaries of photojournalists in these other cities. The Newspaper Guild reports the following minimum salary information for reporters and photographers as of April 1, 2000:

Newspaper	Weekly Salary	Annual Salary	Salary Equivalent to Ohio	Change in Buying Power
New York Times	$1,158.96	$60,266	$49,720	+$10,546
Los Angeles Daily News	$707.00	$36,764•	$29,044	−$4,344
Minneapolis Star Tribune	$1081.75	$56,251*	$24,382	+$1,138
Cleveland Plain Dealer	$1077.21	$56,014.92*	—	—

* = after 5 yrs.   • = after 6 yrs.

If you moved to New York City and secured employment at the *New York Times*, you would be able to maintain a lifestyle similar to the one you led in Cleveland; in fact, you would even be able to enhance your lifestyle given the increase in buying power. The same would not be true for a move to Los Angeles or Minneapolis. You would decrease your buying power given the rate of pay and cost of living in these cities.

....

You can work through a similar exercise for any type of job you are considering and for many locations when current salary information is available. It will be worth your time to undertake this analysis if you are seriously considering a relocation. By doing so you will be able to make an informed choice.

STEP 4 Exploring Your Longer-Term Goals

There is no question that when we first begin working, our goals are to use our skills and education in a job that will reward us with employment, income, and status relative to the preparation we brought with us to this position. If we are not being paid as much as we feel we should for our level of education or if job demands don't provide the intellectual stimulation we had hoped for, we experience unhappiness and as a result often seek other employment.

Most jobs we consider "good" are those that fulfill our basic "lower-level" needs of security, food, clothing, shelter, income, and productive work. But even when our basic needs are met and our jobs are secure and productive, we as individuals are constantly changing. As we change, the demands and expectations we place on our jobs may change. Fortunately, some jobs grow and change with us, and this explains why some people are happy throughout many years in a job.

But more often people are bigger than the jobs they fill. We have more goals and needs than any job could satisfy. These are "higher-level" needs of self-esteem, companionship, affection, and an increasing desire to feel we are employing ourselves in the most effective way possible. Not all of these higher-level needs can be met through employment, but for as long as we are employed, we increasingly demand that our jobs play their part in moving us along the path to fulfillment.

Another obvious but important fact is that we change as we mature. Although our jobs also have the potential for change, they may not change as frequently or as markedly as we do. There are increasingly fewer one-job, one-employer careers; we must think about a work future that may involve voluntary or forced moves from employer to employer. Because of that very real possibility, we need to take advantage of the opportunities in each position we hold to acquire skills and competencies that will keep us viable and attractive as employees in a job market that not only is technology/computer dependent, but also is populated with more and more small, self-transforming organizations rather than the large, seemingly stable organizations of the past.

It may be difficult in the early stages of the job search to determine whether the path you are considering can meet these longer-term goals. Reading about career paths and individual career histories in your field can be very helpful in this regard. Meeting and talking with individuals further along in their careers can be enlightening as well. Older workers can provide valuable guidance on "self-managing" your career, which will become an increasingly valuable skill in the future. Some of these ideas may seem remote as you read this now, but you should be able to appreciate the need to ensure that you are growing, developing valuable new skills, and researching other employers who might be interested in your particular skills package.

· ·

If you are considering a position in advertising, for example, you would gain a far better perspective of your potential future if you could talk to an entry-level account assistant, a more experienced account executive, and, finally, an account supervisor with a significant work history in advertising. Each will have a different perspective, unique concerns, and an individual set of value priorities.

· ·

STEP 5   Enumerating Your Skill Base

In terms of the job search, skills can be thought of as capabilities that can be developed in school, at work, or by volunteering and then used in specific job settings. Many studies have documented the kinds of skills that employers seek in entry-level applicants. For example, some of the most desired skills for individuals interested in the teaching profession are the ability to interact effectively with students one-on-one, to manage a classroom, to adapt to varying situations as necessary, and to get involved in school activities. Business employers have also identified important qualities, including enthusiasm for the employer's product or service, a businesslike mind, the ability to follow written or oral instructions, the ability to demonstrate self-control, the confidence to suggest new ideas, the ability to communicate with all members of a group, an awareness of cultural differences, and loyalty, to name just a few. You will find that many of these skills are also in the repertoire of qualities demanded in your college major.

To be successful in obtaining any given job, you must be able to demonstrate that you possess a certain mix of skills that will allow you to carry out the duties required by that job. This skill mix will vary a great deal from job to job; to determine the skills necessary for the jobs you are seeking, you can read job advertisements or more generic job descriptions, such as those found later in this book. If you want to be effective in the job search, you must directly show employers that you possess the skills needed to be successful in filling the position. These skills will initially be described on your resume and then discussed again during the interview process.

Skills are either general or specific. General skills are those that are developed throughout your college years by taking classes, being employed, and getting involved in other related activities such as volunteer work or campus organizations. General skills include the ability to read and write, to perform computations, to think critically, and to communicate effectively. Specific skills are also acquired on the job and in the classroom, but they allow you to complete tasks that require specialized knowledge. Computer programming, drafting, language translating, and copyediting are just a few examples of specific skills that may relate to a given job.

To develop a list of skills relevant to employers, you must first identify the general skills you possess, then list specific skills you have to offer, and, finally, examine which of these skills employers are seeking.

Identifying Your General Skills. Because you possess or will possess a college degree, employers will assume that you can read and write, perform certain basic computations, think critically, and communicate effectively. Employers will want to see that you have acquired these skills, and they will want to know which additional general skills you possess.

One way to begin identifying skills is to write an experiential diary. An experiential diary lists all the tasks you were responsible for completing for each job you've held and then outlines the skills required to do those tasks. You may list several skills for any given task. This diary allows you to distinguish between the tasks you performed and the underlying skills required to complete those tasks. Here's an example:

Tasks	Skills
Answering telephone	Effective use of language, clear diction, ability to direct inquiries, ability to solve problems
Waiting on tables	Poise under conditions of time and pressure, speed, accuracy, good memory, simultaneous completion of tasks, sales skills

For each job or experience you have participated in, develop a worksheet based on the example shown here. On a resume, you may want to describe these skills rather than simply listing tasks. Skills are easier for the employer to appreciate, especially when your experience is very different from the employment you are seeking. In addition to helping you identify general skills, this experiential diary will prepare you to speak more effectively in an interview about the qualifications you possess.

Identifying Your Specific Skills. It may be easier to identify your specific skills because you can definitely say whether you can speak other languages, program a computer, draft a map or diagram, or edit a document using appropriate symbols and terminology.

Using your experiential diary, identify the points in your history where you learned how to do something very specific, and decide whether you have a beginning, intermediate, or advanced knowledge of how to use that particular skill. Right now, be sure to list *every* specific skill you have, and don't consider whether you like using the skill. Write down a list of specific skills you have acquired and the level of competence you possess—beginning, intermediate, or advanced.

Relating Your Skills to Employers. You probably have thought about a couple of different jobs you might be interested in obtaining, and one way to begin relating the general and specific skills you possess to a potential employer's needs is to read actual advertisements for these types of positions (see Part Two for resources listing actual job openings).

• •

For example, you might be interested in a career as a senior editor for a magazine. A typical job listing might read, "Requires 2–5 years experience, organizational and interpersonal skills, imagination, drive, and the ability to work under pressure." If you then used any one of a number of general sources of information that describe the job of senior editor, you would find additional information. Senior editors also develop story ideas, make assignments, work with staff and freelance writers, edit articles, and coordinate with other magazine departments, including the art department and sales.

Begin building a comprehensive list of required skills with the first job description you read. Exploring advertisements for and descriptions of several types of related positions will reveal an important core of skills that is necessary for obtaining the type of work in which you're interested. In building this list, include both general and specific skills.

Following is a sample list of skills needed to be successful as a senior editor for a magazine. These items were extracted from general resources and actual job listings:

JOB: SENIOR EDITOR FOR A MAGAZINE

General Skills	Specific Skills
Disseminate information	Write editorials
Gather information	Take notes
Conduct research	Write letters
Work in hectic environment	Write memos
Meet deadlines	Use tape recorder
Work long hours near deadline	Develop story ideas
Work well with other people	Assign articles
Exhibit creativity	Edit articles
Exhibit drive	Schedule articles
Be able to work under pressure	Proofread
Be organized	Familiar with word
Be able to supervise the work	processing
of others	Lay out pages
Have excellent written and verbal	Select illustrations
skills	
Be able to conduct meetings	

On a separate sheet of paper, try to generate a comprehensive list of required skills for at least one job that you are considering.

The list of general skills that you develop for a given career path would be valuable for any number of jobs for which you might apply. Many of the specific skills would also be transferable to other types of positions. For example, developing story ideas is a required skill for magazine editors, and it would also be a required skill for senior editors working on a newspaper.

....

Now review the list of skills that are required for jobs you are considering, and check off those skills that *you know you possess*. You should refer to these specific skills on the resume that you write for this type of job. See Chapter 2 for details on resume writing.

STEP 6 Recognizing Your Preferred Skills

In the previous section you developed a comprehensive list of skills that relate to particular career paths that are of interest to you. You can now relate these to skills that you prefer to use. We all use a wide range of skills (some researchers say individuals have a repertoire of about 500 skills), but we may not be particularly interested in using all of them in our work. There may be some skills that come to us more naturally or that we use successfully time and time again and that we want to continue to use; these are best described as our preferred skills. For this exercise use the list of skills that you created for the previous section, and decide which of them you are *most interested in using* in future work and how often you would like to use them. You might be interested in using some skills only occasionally, while others you would like to use more regularly. You probably also have skills that you hope you can use constantly.

As you examine job announcements, look for matches between this list of preferred skills and the qualifications described in the advertisements. These skills should be highlighted on your resume and discussed in job interviews.

STEP 7 Assessing Skills Needing Further Development

Previously you compiled a list of general and specific skills required for given positions. You already possess some of these skills; those that remain to be developed are your underdeveloped skills.

If you are just beginning the job search, there may be gaps between the qualifications required for some of the jobs you're considering and skills you possess. The thought of having to admit to and talk about these underdeveloped skills, especially in a job interview, is a frightening one. One way to put a healthy perspective on this subject is to target and relate your exploration of underdeveloped skills to the types of positions you are seeking. Recognizing these shortcomings and planning to overcome them with either on-the-job training or additional formal education can be a positive way to address the concept of underdeveloped skills.

On your worksheet or in your journal, make a list of up to five general or specific skills required for the positions you're interested in that you *don't currently possess*. For each item list an idea you have for specific action you could take to acquire that skill. Do some brainstorming to come up with possible actions. If you have a hard time generating ideas, talk to people currently working in this type of position, professionals in your college career services office, trusted friends, family members, or members of related professional associations.

If, for example, you are interested in a job for which you don't have some specific required experience, you could locate training opportunities such as classes or workshops offered through a local college or university, community college, or club or association that would help you build the level of expertise you need for the job.

You will notice in this book that many excellent positions for your major demand computer skills. While basic word processing has been something you've done all through college, you may be surprised at the additional computer skills required by employers. Many positions for college graduates will ask for some familiarity with spreadsheet programming, and frequently some database-management software familiarity is a job demand as well. Desktop publishing software, graphics programs, and basic Web-page design also pop up frequently in job ads for college graduates. If your degree program hasn't introduced you to a wide variety of computer applications, what are your options? If you're still in college, take what computer courses you can before you graduate. If you've already graduated, look at evening programs, continuing education courses, or tutorial programs that may be available commercially. Developing a modest level of expertise will encourage you to be more confident in suggesting to potential employers that you can continue to add to your skill base on the job.

In Chapter 5 on interviewing, we will discuss in detail how to effectively address questions about underdeveloped skills. Generally speaking, though, employers want genuine answers to these types of questions. They want you to reveal "the real you," and they also want to see how you answer difficult questions. In taking the positive, targeted approach discussed above, you show the employer that you are willing to continue to learn and that you have a plan for strengthening your job qualifications.

USING YOUR SELF-ASSESSMENT

Exploring entry-level career options can be an exciting experience if you have good resources available and will take the time to use them. Can you effectively complete the following tasks?

1. Understand your personality traits and relate them to career choices

2. Define your personal values

3. Determine your economic needs

4. Explore longer-term goals

5. Understand your skill base

6. Recognize your preferred skills

7. Express a willingness to improve on your underdeveloped skills

If so, then you can more meaningfully participate in the job search process by writing a more effective resume, finding job titles that represent work you are interested in doing, locating job sites that will provide the opportunity for you to use your strengths and skills, networking in an informed way, participating in focused interviews, getting the most out of follow-up contacts, and evaluating job offers to find those that create a good match between you and the employer. The remaining chapters in Part One guide you through these next steps in the job search process. For many job seekers, this process can take anywhere from three months to a year to implement. The time you will need to put into your job search will depend on the type of job you want and the geographic location where you'd like to work. Think of your effort as a job in itself, requiring you to set aside time each week to complete the needed work. Carefully undertaken efforts may reduce the time you need for your job search.

CHAPTER TWO

THE RESUME AND COVER LETTER

The task of writing a resume may seem overwhelming if you are unfamiliar with this type of document, but there are some easily understood techniques that can and should be used. This section was written to help you understand the purpose of the resume, the different types of resume formats available, and how to write the sections of information traditionally found on a resume. We will present examples and explanations that address questions frequently posed by people writing their first resume or updating an old resume.

Even within the formats and suggestions given, however, there are infinite variations. True, most resumes follow one of the outlines suggested, but you should feel free to adjust the resume to suit your needs and make it expressive of your life and experience.

WHY WRITE A RESUME?

The purpose of a resume is to convince an employer that you should be interviewed. Whether you're mailing, faxing, or E-mailing this document, you'll want to present enough information to show that you can make an immediate and valuable contribution to an organization. A resume is not an in-depth historical or legal document; later in the job search process you may be asked to document your entire work history on an application form and attest to its validity. The resume should, instead, highlight relevant information pertaining directly to the organization that will receive the document or to the type of position you are seeking.

We will discuss four types of resumes in this chapter: chronological, functional, targeted, and digital. The reasons for using one type of resume over another and the typical format for each are addressed in the following sections.

THE CHRONOLOGICAL RESUME

The chronological resume is the most common of the various resume formats and therefore the format that employers are most used to receiving. This type of resume is easy to read and understand because it details the chronological progression of jobs you have held. (See Exhibit 2.1.) It begins with your most recent employment and works back in time. If you have a solid work history or have experience that provided growth and development in your duties and responsibilities, a chronological resume will highlight these achievements. The typical elements of a chronological resume include the heading, a career objective, educational background, employment experience, activities, and references.

The Heading
The heading consists of your name, address, telephone number, and other means of contact. This may include a fax number, E-mail address, and your home-page address. If you are using a shared E-mail account or a parent's business fax, be sure to let others who use these systems know that you may receive important professional correspondence via these systems. You wouldn't want to miss a vital E-mail or fax! Likewise, if your resume directs readers to a personal home page on the Web, be certain it's a professional personal home page designed to be viewed and appreciated by a prospective employer. This may mean making substantial changes in the home page you currently mount on the Web.

We suggest that you spell out your full name in your resume heading and type it in all capital letters in bold type. After all, you are the focus of the resume! If you have a current as well as a permanent address and you include both in the heading, be sure to indicate until what date your current address will be valid. The two-letter state abbreviation should be the only abbreviation that appears in your heading. Don't forget to include the zip code with your address and the area code with your telephone number.

The Objective
As you formulate the wording for this part of your resume, keep the following points in mind.

Exhibit 2.1

CHRONOLOGICAL RESUME

BARBARA O'NEIL

Apartment 6	14 Fleming Street
Boston University	Apartment 26A
Boston, MA 01851	Key West, FL 98766
(617) 555-5555	(723) 555-5555
boneil@xxx.com	
(until May 2003)	

OBJECTIVE
A career in publishing, initially as an editor and ultimately as a managing editor

EDUCATION
Bachelor of Arts in Communications
Boston University
May 2003
Minor: English

HONORS/AWARDS
Chancellor's Scholar, Spring/Fall Semesters, 2000
Who's Who Among Universities and Colleges, 2001–2002
The *BU Daily* Student Reporting Award, 1999

RELATED COURSES

Publishing Law	Media and the Marketplace
Ethics in Publishing	Creative Writing

EXPERIENCE
Tutor, Academic Support Services, Boston University. Part-time, 2000–2001. Taught students basic composition skills, organizing material, writing effective openings and conclusions.
Staff Assistant, Little, Brown & Co., Boston, MA. Summers 1999–2001. Editorial department, trade hardcover division. Proofread and edited manuscripts for publication.
Staff Assistant, *Boston Globe,* Boston, MA. Part-time, 1999–2000. Work-study job as one of five assistants for a major newspaper. Assisted travel editor screening freelance submissions and press releases. Editing and proofreading.

ACTIVITIES
Yearbook Production Staff, Boston University, 1999–present.
Evening with an Author Program, 1999–present. Arrange for guest speakers, act as escort, coordinate accommodations and transportation.

REFERENCES
Available upon request.

The Objective Focuses the Resume. Without a doubt this is the most challenging part of the resume for most resume writers. Even for individuals who have decided on a career path, it can be difficult to encapsulate all they want to say in one or two brief sentences. For job seekers who are unfocused or unclear about their intentions, trying to write this section can inhibit the entire resume writing process.

Recruiters tell us time and time again that the objective creates a frame of reference for them. It helps them see how you express your goals and career focus. In addition, the statement may indicate in what ways you can immediately benefit an organization. Given the importance of the objective, every point covered in the resume should relate to it. If information doesn't relate, it should be omitted. You'll file a number of resume variations in your computer. There's no excuse for not being able to tailor a resume to individual employers or specific positions.

Choose an Appropriate Length. Because of the brevity necessary for a resume, you should keep the objective as short as possible. Although objectives of only four or five words often don't show much direction, objectives that take three full lines could be viewed as too wordy and might possibly be ignored.

Consider Which Type of Objective Statement You Will Use. There are many ways to state an objective, but generally there are four forms this statement can take: (1) a very general statement; (2) a statement focused on a specific position; (3) a statement focused on a specific industry; or (4) a summary of your qualifications. In our contacts with employers, we often hear that many resumes don't exhibit any direction or career goals, so we suggest avoiding general statements when possible.

1. General Objective Statement. General objective statements look like the following:

- An entry-level educational programming coordinator position
- An entry-level marketing position

This type of objective would be useful if you know what type of job you want but you're not sure which industries interest you.

2. Position-Focused Objective.
Following are examples of objectives focusing on a specific position:

- To obtain the position of conference coordinator at State College
- To obtain a position as assistant editor at *Time* magazine

When a student applies for an advertised job opening, this type of focus can be very effective. The employer knows that the applicant has taken the time to tailor the resume specifically for this position.

3. Industry-Focused Objective.
Focusing on a particular industry in an objective could be stated as follows:

- To begin a career as a sales representative in the cruise line industry

4. Summary of Qualifications Statement.
The summary of qualifications can be used instead of an objective or in conjunction with an objective. The purpose of this type of statement is to highlight relevant qualifications gained through a variety of experiences. This type of statement is often used by individuals with extensive and diversified work experience. An example of a qualifications statement follows:

··

A degree in communications and four years of progressively increasing job responsibility within the publishing industry have prepared me to begin a career as an editor with an organization that values hard work and dedication.

··

Support Your Objective. A resume that contains any one of these types of objective statements should then go on to demonstrate why you are qualified to get the position. Listing academic degrees can be one way to indicate qualifications. Another demonstration would be in the way previous experiences, both volunteer and paid, are described. Without this kind of documentation in the body of the resume, the objective looks unsupported.

Think of the resume as telling a connected story about you. All the elements should work together to form a coherent picture that ideally should relate to your statement of objective.

Education

This section of your resume should indicate the exact name of the degree you will receive or have received, spelled out completely with no abbreviations. The degree is generally listed after the objective, followed by the institution name and location, and then the month and year of graduation. This section could also include your academic minor, grade point average (GPA), and appearance on the Dean's List or President's List.

If you have enough space, you might want to include a section listing courses related to the field in which you are seeking work. The best use of a "related courses" section would be to list some course work that is not traditionally associated with the major. Perhaps you took several computer courses outside your degree that will be helpful and related to the job prospects you are entertaining. Several education section examples are shown here:

• •

- Bachelor of Arts in Communication Studies
  UCLA, Los Angeles, CA, December 2001
  Minor: Community Health

- Bachelor of Arts in Communication Disorders, specializing in industrial settings, Tufts University, Medford, MA, May 2001

- Bachelor of Arts in Health Communications, Columbia University, New York City, NY, May 2001

An example of a format for a related courses section follows:

RELATED COURSES	
Campaign Promotions	Public Relations
Public Speaking	Group Interaction
Intercollegiate Forensics	Problem Solving

• •

Experience

The experience section of your resume should be the most substantial part and should take up most of the space on the page. Employers want to see what kind of work history you have. They will look at your range of experiences, longevity in jobs, and specific tasks you are able to complete. This section may also be called "work experience," "related experience," "employment history," or "employment." No matter what you call this section, some important points to remember are the following:

1. **Describe your duties** as they relate to the position you are seeking.

2. **Emphasize major responsibilities** and indicate increases in responsibility. Include all relevant employment experiences: summer, part-time, internships, cooperative education, or self-employment.

3. **Emphasize skills,** especially those that transfer from one situation to another. The fact that you coordinated a student organization, chaired meetings, supervised others, and managed a budget leads one to suspect that you could coordinate other things as well.

4. **Use descriptive job titles** that provide information about what you did. A "Student Intern" should be more specifically stated as, for example, "Magazine Operations Intern." "Volunteer" is also too general; a title such as "Peer Writing Tutor" would be more appropriate.

5. **Create word pictures** by using active verbs to start sentences. Describe *results* you have produced in the work you have done.

A limp description would say something such as the following: "My duties included helping with production, proofreading, and editing. I used a word-processing package to alter text." An action statement would be stated as follows: "Coordinated and assisted in the creative marketing of brochures and seminar promotions, becoming proficient in Word."

Remember, an accomplishment is simply a result, a final measurable product that people can relate to. A duty is not a result; it is an obligation—every job holder has duties. For an effective resume, list as many results as you can. To make the most of the limited space you have and to give your description impact, carefully select appropriate and accurate descriptors from the list of action words in Exhibit 2.2.

Here are some traits that employers tell us they like to see:

■ Teamwork

■ Energy and motivation

Exhibit 2.2

RESUME ACTION VERBS

Achieved	Drafted	Mapped
Acted	Edited	Marketed
Administered	Eliminated	Met
Advised	Ensured	Modified
Analyzed	Established	Monitored
Assessed	Estimated	Negotiated
Assisted	Evaluated	Observed
Attained	Examined	Obtained
Balanced	Explained	Operated
Budgeted	Facilitated	Organized
Calculated	Finalized	Participated
Collected	Generated	Performed
Communicated	Handled	Planned
Compiled	Headed	Predicted
Completed	Helped	Prepared
Composed	Identified	Presented
Conceptualized	Illustrated	Processed
Condensed	Implemented	Produced
Conducted	Improved	Projected
Consolidated	Increased	Proposed
Constructed	Influenced	Provided
Controlled	Informed	Qualified
Converted	Initiated	Quantified
Coordinated	Innovated	Questioned
Corrected	Instituted	Realized
Created	Instructed	Received
Decreased	Integrated	Recommended
Defined	Interpreted	Recorded
Demonstrated	Introduced	Reduced
Designed	Learned	Reinforced
Determined	Lectured	Reported
Developed	Led	Represented
Directed	Maintained	Researched
Documented	Managed	Resolved

Reviewed	Sold	Systematized
Scheduled	Solved	Tabulated
Selected	Staffed	Tested
Served	Streamlined	Transacted
Showed	Studied	Updated
Simplified	Submitted	Verified
Sketched	Summarized	

- Learning and using new skills

- Versatility

- Critical thinking

- Understanding how profits are created

- Organizational acumen

- Communicating directly and clearly, in both writing and speaking

- Risk taking

- Willingness to admit mistakes

- High personal standards

SOLUTIONS TO FREQUENTLY ENCOUNTERED PROBLEMS

Repetitive Employment with the Same Employer

EMPLOYMENT: The Foot Locker, Portland, Oregon. Summer 2001, 2002, 2003. Initially employed in high school as salesclerk. Due to successful performance, asked to return next two summers at higher pay with added responsibility. Ranked as the #2 salesperson the first summer and #1 the next two summers. Assisted in arranging eye-catching retail displays; served as manager of other summer workers during owner's absence.

A Large Number of Jobs

EMPLOYMENT: Recent Hospitality Industry Experience: Affiliated with four upscale hotel/restaurant complexes (September 2001–February 2004), where I worked part- and full-time as a waiter, bartender, disc jockey, and bookkeeper to produce income for college.

Several Positions with the Same Employer

EMPLOYMENT: Coca-Cola Bottling Co., Burlington, Vermont, 2001–2004. In four years, I received three promotions, each with increased pay and responsibility.

Summer Sales Coordinator: Promoted to hire, train, and direct efforts of add-on staff of fifteen college-age route salespeople hired to meet summer peak demand for product.

Sales Administrator: Promoted to run home office sales desk, managing accounts and associated delivery schedules for professional sales force of ten people. Intensive phone work, daily interaction with all personnel, and strong knowledge of product line required.

Route Salesperson: Summer employment to travel and tourism industry sites that use Coke products. Met specific schedule demands, used good communication skills with wide variety of customers, and demonstrated strong selling skills. Named salesperson of the month for July and August of that year.

QUESTIONS RESUME WRITERS OFTEN ASK

How Far Back Should I Go in Terms of Listing Past Jobs?

Usually, listing three or four jobs should suffice. If you did something back in high school that has a bearing on your future aspirations for employment, by all means list the job. As you progress through your college career, high school jobs will be replaced on the resume by college employment.

Should I Differentiate Between Paid and Nonpaid Employment?

Most employers are not initially concerned about how much you were paid. They are eager to know how much responsibility you held in your past employment. There is no need to specify that your work was as a volunteer if you had significant responsibilities.

How Should I Represent My Accomplishments or Work-Related Responsibilities?

Succinctly, but fully. In other words, give the employer enough information to arouse curiosity but not so much detail that you leave nothing to the imagination. Besides, some jobs merit more lengthy explanations than others. Be sure to convey any information that can give an employer a better understanding of the depth of your involvement at work. Did you supervise others? How many? Did your efforts result in a more efficient operation? How much did you increase efficiency? Did you handle a budget? How much? Were you promoted in a short time? Did you work two jobs at once or fifteen hours per week after high school? Where appropriate, quantify.

Should the Work Section Always Follow the Education Section on the Resume?

Always lead with your strengths. If your education closely relates to the employment you now seek, put this section after the objective. Or, if you are weak on the academic side but have a surplus of good work experiences, consider reversing the order of your sections to lead with employment, followed by education.

How Should I Present My Activities, Honors, Awards, Professional Societies, and Affiliations?

This section of the resume can add valuable information for an employer to consider if used correctly. The rule of thumb for information in this section is to include only those activities that are in some way relevant to the objective stated on your resume. If you can draw a valid connection between your activities and your objective, include them; if not, leave them out.

Granted, this is hard to do. Playing center on the championship basketball team or serving as coordinator of the biggest homecoming parade ever held are roles that have meaning for you and represent personal accomplishments you'd like to share. But the resume is a brief document, and the information you provide on it should help the employer make a decision about your job eligibility. Including personal details can be confusing and could hurt your candidacy. Limiting your activity list to a few significant experiences can be very effective.

If you are applying for a position as a safety officer, your certificate in Red Cross lifesaving skills or CPR would be related and valuable. You would want to include it. If, however, you are applying for a job as a junior account executive in an advertising agency, that information would be unrelated and superfluous. Leave it out.

Professional affiliations and honors should all be listed; especially important are those related to your job objective. Social clubs and activities need not be a part of your resume unless you hold a significant office or you are looking for a position related to your membership. Be aware that most prospective employers' principal concerns are related to your employability, not your social life. If you have any, publications can be included as an addendum to your resume.

The focus of the resume is your experience and education. It is not necessary to describe your involvement in activities. However, if your resume needs to be lengthened, this section provides the freedom either to expand on or mention only briefly the contributions you have made. If you have made significant contributions (e.g., an officer of an organization or a particularly long tenure with a group), you may choose to describe them in more detail. It is not always necessary to include the dates of your memberships with your activities the way you would include job dates.

There are various ways in which to present additional information. You may give this section a number of different titles. Assess what you want to list, and then use an appropriate title. Do not use "extracurricular activities." This terminology is scholastic, not professional, and therefore not appropriate. The following are two examples:

- ACTIVITIES: Society for Technical Communication, Student Senate, Student Admissions Representative, Senior Class Officer

- ACTIVITIES:
  - Society for Technical Communication Member
  - Student Senator
  - Student Admissions Representative
  - Senior Class Officer

The position you are looking for will determine what you should or should not include. *Always* look for a correlation between the activity and the prospective job.

How Should I Handle References?

The use of references is considered a part of the interview process, and they should never be listed on a resume. You would always provide references to a potential employer if requested to, so it is not even necessary to include this section on the resume if space does not permit. If space is available, it is acceptable to include one of the following statements:

- REFERENCES: Furnished upon request.

- REFERENCES: Available upon request.

Individuals used as references must be protected from unnecessary contacts. By including names on your resume, you leave your references unprotected. Overuse and abuse of your references will lead to less-than-supportive comments. Protect your references by giving out their names only when you are being considered seriously as a candidate for a given position.

THE FUNCTIONAL RESUME

The functional resume departs from a chronological resume in that it organizes information by specific accomplishments in various settings: previous jobs, volunteer work, associations, and so forth. This type of resume permits you to stress the substance of your experiences rather than the position titles you have held. (See Exhibit 2.3.) You should consider using a functional resume if you have held a series of similar jobs that relied on the same skills or abilities.

The Objective

A functional resume begins with an objective that can be used to focus the contents of the resume.

Specific Accomplishments

Specific accomplishments are listed on this type of resume. Examples of the types of headings used to describe these capabilities might include research, computer skills, teaching, communication, production, management, marketing, or writing. The headings you choose will directly relate to your experience and the tasks that you carried out. Each accomplishment section contains statements related to your experience in that category, regardless of when or where it occurred. Organize the accomplishments and the related tasks you describe in their order of importance as related to the position you seek.

Experience or Employment History

Your actual work experience is condensed and placed after the specific accomplishments section. It simply lists dates of employment, position titles, and employer names.

Education

The education section of a functional resume is identical to that of the chronological resume, but it does not carry the same visual importance because it is placed near the bottom of the page.

References

Because actual reference names are never listed on a resume, a statement of reference availability is optional.

Exhibit 2.3

FUNCTIONAL RESUME

CARLOS HIDALGO

Student Apartment 12
Florida Atlantic University
Boca Raton, FL 33424
(407) 555-5555
Fax (407) 555-5556
chidalgo@xxx.com
(until May 2003)

12 Cornwall Street
Rocky River, OH 44116
(212) 555-5555

OBJECTIVE
An entry-level assistant account executive position that allows me to show my initiative and use my copywriting and design skills

CAPABILITIES
• Creative copywriting
• Team player
• Design techniques

SELECTED ACCOMPLISHMENTS
Copywriting: Created headlines and leads for national advertising campaigning; wrote copy for print and direct mail advertising for magazine subscriptions; researched competitive products and services; wrote and designed flyers for bookstore events; helped select photographs, line drawings, and other illustrations for variety of print ads.

Team Player: Collaborated with coworkers and professionals in other departments on national advertising campaign. Worked closely with designers, artists, and photographers. Participated in account meetings.

Design Techniques: Familiar with computer graphics, CAD, and desktop publishing programs. Assisted in layout and design of various print and direct mail advertisements.

AWARDS
Graduated with Honors
Nominated to National Honor Society
Received Outstanding Part-Time Employee of the Year Award

EMPLOYMENT HISTORY
Account Executive Intern, M & L Design Studio, West Palm Beach, Florida,
Summers, 2001–2003
Clerk and Assistant Events Coordinator, FAU Bookstore, Florida Atlantic University,
Boca Raton, Florida, Summers, 1999–Present

EDUCATION
Bachelor of Arts in Communications
Florida Atlantic University, Boca Raton, Florida
May 2003

REFERENCES
Provided upon request.

THE TARGETED RESUME

The targeted resume focuses on specific work-related capabilities you can bring to a given position within an organization. (See Exhibit 2.4.) It should be sent to an individual within the organization who makes hiring decisions about the position you are seeking.

The Objective
The objective on this type of resume should be targeted to a specific career or position. It should be supported by the capabilities, accomplishments, and achievements documented in the resume.

Capabilities
Capabilities should be statements that illustrate tasks you believe you are capable of based on your accomplishments, achievements, and work history. Each should relate to your targeted career or position. You can stress your qualifications rather than your employment history. This approach may require research to obtain an understanding of the nature of the work involved and the capabilities necessary to carry out that work.

Accomplishments/Achievements
This section relates the various activities you have been involved in to the job market. These experiences may include previous jobs, extracurricular activities at school, internships, and part-time summer work.

Experience

Your work history should be listed in abbreviated form and may include position title, employer name, and employment dates.

Education

Because this type of resume is directed toward a specific job target and an individual's related experience, the education section is not prominently located at the top of the resume as is done on the chronological resume.

DIGITAL RESUMES

Today's employers have to manage an enormous number of resumes. One of the most frequent complaints the writers of this series hear from students is the failure of employers to even acknowledge the receipt of a resume and cover letter. Frequently, the reason for this poor response or nonresponse is the volume of applications received for every job. In an attempt to better manage the considerable labor investment involved in processing large numbers of resumes, many employers are requiring digital submission of resumes. There are two types of digital resumes: those that can be E-mailed or posted to a website, called *electronic resumes*, and those that can be "read" by a computer, commonly called *scannable resumes*. Though the format may be a bit different from the traditional "paper" resume, the goal of both types of digital resumes is the same—to get you an interview! These resumes must be designed to be "technologically friendly." What that basically means to you is that they should be free of graphics and fancy formatting.

Electronic Resumes

Sometimes referred to as plain-text resumes, electronic resumes are designed to be E-mailed to an employer or posted to a commercial Internet database such as CareerMosaic.com, America's Job Bank (www.ajb.dni.us), or Monster.com.

Some technical considerations:

- Electronic resumes must be written in American Standard Code for Information Interchange (ASCII), which is simply a plain-text format. These characters are universally recognized so that every computer can accurately read and understand them. To create an ASCII file of your current resume, open your document, then save it as a text or ASCII file. This will eliminate all formatting. Edit as needed using your computer's text editor application.

Exhibit 2.4

TARGETED RESUME

AMANDA BAILEY

Student Apartment 2A
Colorado State University
Fort Collins, CO 80231
(303) 555-5555
Fax (303) 555-5556
manda@xxx.com
(until May 2004)

43 London Street
Rosendale, NY 12472
(914) 555-5555

JOB TARGET
Promotional campaign manager with local or state service

CAPABILITIES
- Research and analyze target audience
- Collaborate with copywriters and designers
- Coordinate efforts with local and national media
- Organize related events with speakers and presentations
- Familiar with a variety of computer software

ACHIEVEMENTS
- Several articles published in local and national newspapers
- Reached fund-raising goal for local humane shelter
- Maintained a 4.0 average throughout college

WORK HISTORY
2003–present *Assistant Campaign Manager*, Fort Collins Big Brother/Big Sister.
(part-time)   Organized promotional events, assisted manager

2001–present *Public Relations Assistant*, Community Hospital. Part-time
              community service work

2001–2002   *Orderly,* Community Hospital. Part-time work assisting medical staff

EDUCATION
Bachelor of Arts in Communications, 2004
Colorado State University, Fort Collins, Colorado
Emphasis: Health Care

- Use a standard-width typeface. Courier is a good choice because it is the font associated with ASCII in most systems.

- Use a font size of 11 to 14 points. A 12-point font is considered standard.

- Your margin should be left-justified.

- Do not exceed sixty-five characters per line because the word-wrap function doesn't operate in ASCII.

- Do not use boldface, italics, underlining, bullets, or various font sizes. Instead, use asterisks, plus signs, or all capital letters when you want to emphasize something.

- Avoid graphics and shading.

- Use as many "keywords" as you possibly can. These are words or phrases usually relating to skills or experience that either are specifically used in the job announcement or are popular buzzwords in the industry.

- Minimize abbreviations.

- Your name should be the first line of text.

- Conduct a "test run" by E-mailing your resume to yourself and a friend before you send it to the employer. See how it transmits, and make any changes you need to. Continue to test it until it's exactly how you want it to look.

- Unless an employer specifically requests that you send the resume in the form of an attachment, don't. Employers can encounter problems opening a document as an attachment, and there are always viruses to consider.

- Don't forget your cover letter. Send it along with your resume as a single message.

Scannable Resumes

Some companies are relying on technology to narrow the candidate pool for available job openings. Electronic Applicant Tracking uses imaging to scan, sort, and store resume elements in a database. Then, through OCR (Optical Character Recognition) software, the computer scans the resumes for keywords and phrases. To have the best chance at getting an interview, you want to increase the number of "hits"—matches of your skills, abilities, experi-

Exhibit 2.5

DIGITAL RESUME

ANDREW TYLER
117 Stetson Avenue
Small School, NV 02459
508-555-5555
atyler@xxx.com

Put your name at the top on its own line.

Put your phone number on its own line.

Use a standard-width typeface.

KEYWORD SUMMARY
B.A. Communications, 2002
Public Relations, Promotional Events,
Copywriting, Publishing,
Graphic Arts, Fund-Raising,
Editor

Keywords make your resume easier to find in a database.

EDUCATION
Bachelor of Arts, Communications, 2002
Small State College, Small School, Nevada
Minor: Graphic Design
G.P.A.: 3.0/4.0

Capital letters emphasize headings.

RELATED COURSES
Public Speaking
Creative Writing
Publishing Law
Media and the Marketplace

No line should exceed sixty-five characters.

SKILL TRAINING
Copywriting, Graphic Design,
Event Coordination

End each line by hitting the ENTER key.

EXPERIENCE
ABC Publishing Company, 2001–2002
* Numerous assignments over two years
* Copyediting and proofreading
* Promoted and increase in salary
* Design and page layout

Use a space between asterisk and text.

continued

Tutor, 1999–2001
* Taught composition skills
* Instructed students on organizing material

House Painting, 2000
* Established business with friends

COLLEGE ATHLETICS
* Played on inter-hall sports teams
* Cocaptain of the football team

REFERENCES
Available upon request.

++ Willing to relocate ++ ← ———————— Asterisks and plus signs replace bullets.

ence, and education to those the computer is scanning for—your resume will get. You can see how critical using the right keywords is for this type of resume.

Technical considerations include:

- Again, do not use boldface (newer systems may read this OK, but many older ones won't), italics, underlining, bullets, shading, graphics, or multiple font sizes. Instead, for emphasis, use asterisks, plus signs, or all capital letters. Minimize abbreviations.

- Use a popular typeface such as Courier, Helvetica, Ariel, or Palatino. Avoid decorative fonts.

- Font size should be between 11 and 14 points.

- Do not compress the spacing between letters.

- Use horizontal and vertical lines sparingly; the computer may misread them as the letters L or I.

- Left-justify the text.

- Do not use parentheses or brackets around telephone numbers, and be sure your phone number is on its own line of text.

- Your name should be the first line of text and on its own line. If your resume is longer than one page, be sure to put your name on the top of all pages.

- Use a traditional resume structure. The chronological format may work best.

- Use nouns that are skill-focused, such as *management, writer,* and *programming*. This is different from traditional paper resumes, which use action-oriented verbs.

- Laser printers produce the finest copies. Avoid dot-matrix printers.

- Use standard, light-colored paper with text on one side only. Since the higher the contrast, the better, your best choice is black ink on white paper.

- Always send original copies. If you must fax, set the fax on fine mode, not standard.

- Do not staple or fold your resume. This can confuse the computer.

- Before you send your scannable resume, be certain the employer uses this technology. If you can't determine this, you may want to send two versions (scannable and traditional) to be sure your resume gets considered.

RESUME PRODUCTION AND OTHER TIPS

An ink-jet printer is the preferred option for printing your resume. Begin by printing just a few copies. You may find a small error or you may simply want to make some changes, and it is less frustrating and less expensive if you print in small batches.

Resume paper color should be carefully chosen. You should consider the types of employers who will receive your resume and the types of positions for which you are applying. Use white or ivory paper for traditional or conservative employers or for higher-level positions.

Black ink on sharp, white paper can be harsh on the reader's eyes. Think about an ivory or cream paper that will provide less contrast and be easier to read. Pink, green, and blue tints should generally be avoided.

Many resume writers buy packages of matching envelopes and cover sheet stationery that, although not absolutely necessary, help convey a professional impression.

If you'll be producing many cover letters at home, be sure you have high-quality printing equipment. Learn standard envelope formats for business, and retain a copy of every cover letter you send out. You can use the copies to take notes of any telephone conversations that may occur.

If attending a job fair, either carry a briefcase or place your resume in a nicely covered legal-size pad holder.

THE COVER LETTER

The cover letter provides you with the opportunity to tailor your resume by telling the prospective employer how you can be a benefit to the organization. It allows you to highlight aspects of your background that are not already discussed in your resume and that might be especially relevant to the organization you are contacting or to the position you are seeking. Every resume should have a cover letter enclosed when you send it out. Unlike the resume, which may be mass-produced, a cover letter is most effective when it is individually prepared and focused on the particular requirements of the organization in question.

A good cover letter should supplement the resume and motivate the reader to review the resume. The format shown in Exhibit 2.6 is only a suggestion to help you decide what information to include in writing a cover letter.

Begin the cover letter with your street address twelve lines down from the top. Leave three to five lines between the date and the name of the person to whom you are addressing the cover letter. Make sure you leave one blank line between the salutation and the body of the letter and between paragraphs. After typing "Sincerely," leave four blank lines and type your name. This should leave plenty of room for your signature. A sample cover letter is shown in Exhibit 2.7.

The following guidelines will help you write good cover letters:

1. Be sure to type your letter neatly; ensure there are no misspellings.

2. Avoid unusual typefaces, such as script.

3. Address the letter to an individual, using the person's name and title. To obtain this information, call the company. If answering a blind newspaper advertisement, address the letter "To Whom It May Concern" or omit the salutation.

4. Be sure your cover letter directly indicates the position you are applying for and tells why you are qualified to fill it.

5. Send the original letter, not a photocopy, with your resume. Keep a copy for your records.

6. Make your cover letter no more than one page.

7. Include a phone number where you can be reached.

8. Avoid trite language and have someone read the letter over to react to its tone, content, and mechanics.

9. For your own information, record the date you send out each letter and resume.

Exhibit 2.6

COVER LETTER FORMAT

Your Street Address
Your Town, State, Zip
Phone Number
Fax Number
E-mail

Date

Name
Title
Organization
Address

Dear _____ :

First Paragraph. In this paragraph state the reason for the letter, name the specific position or type of work you are applying for, and indicate from which resource (career services office, website, newspaper, contact, employment service) you learned of this opening. The first paragraph can also be used to inquire about future openings.

Second Paragraph. Indicate why you are interested in this position, the company, or its products or services, and what you can do for the employer. If you are a recent graduate, explain how your academic background makes you a qualified candidate. Try not to repeat the same information found in the resume.

Third Paragraph. Refer the reader to the enclosed resume for more detailed information.

Fourth Paragraph. In this paragraph say what you will do to follow up on your letter. For example, state that you will call by a certain date to set up an interview or to find out if the company will be recruiting in your area. Finish by indicating your willingness to answer any questions they may have. Be sure you have provided your phone number.

Sincerely,

Type your name
Enclosure

Exhibit 2.7

SAMPLE COVER LETTER

143 Random Way
Tempe, AZ 85284
(602) 555-3333
Fax (602) 555-5556
rmcneal@xxx.com
March 15, 2002

Ms. Alison Kahn
Director of Human Resources
Southwest Advertising
279 Main Street
Tempe, AZ 85284

Dear Ms. Kahn:

In May of 2003 I will graduate from Arizona State University with a Bachelor of Arts in Communications. I read of your opening for an assistant account executive in *The News*, and I am very interested in the possibilities it offers. I am writing to explore the opportunity for employment with your company.

The ad indicated that you were looking for creative individuals with high energy and good communication skills. I believe I possess those qualities. Through my work with the baby-sitting service I started, I learned the importance of a good imagination and maintaining a positive attitude toward the children and their parents. In addition to the various communications classes in my academic program, I felt it important to enroll in some art and computer courses, such as photography, computer graphics, and computer-assisted design. These courses helped me become comfortable in my interactions with other people and with the world of advertising in general. These traits will help me to represent Southwest Advertising in a professional and enthusiastic manner.

As you will see by my enclosed resume, I worked on the campus newspaper for three years selling advertising space. This position provided me with experience dealing with customers and their needs and allowed me to see how both sides function together.

I would like to meet with you to discuss how my education and experience would be consistent with your needs. I will contact your office next week to discuss the possibility of an interview. In the meantime, if you have any questions or require additional information, please contact me at my home, (602) 555-3333.

Sincerely,

Robin McNeal
Enclosure

CHAPTER THREE

RESEARCHING CAREERS

....

One common question a career counselor encounters is "What should I do with my degree?" Communications majors often struggle with this problem because, unlike their fellow students in more applied fields, such as accounting, computer science, or health and physical education, the job possibilities are vast as are the kinds of organizations that hire for those positions. An accounting major becomes an accountant. A computer science major can apply for a job as a data analyst. But what does a communications major become?

....

WHAT DO THEY CALL THE JOB YOU WANT?

There is every reason to be unaware. One reason for confusion is perhaps a mistaken assumption that a college education provides job training. In most cases it does not. Of course, applied fields such as engineering, management, or education provide specific skills for the workplace, whereas most liberal arts degrees simply provide an education. A liberal arts education exposes you to numerous fields of study and teaches you quantitative reasoning, critical thinking, writing, and speaking, all of which can be successfully applied to a number of different job fields. But it still remains up to you to choose a job field and to learn how to articulate the benefits of your education in a way the employer will appreciate.

As indicated in Chapter 1 on self-assessment, your first task is to understand and value what parts of that education you enjoyed and were good at and would continue to enjoy in your life's work. Did your writing courses encourage you in your ability to express yourself in writing? Did you enjoy the research process, and did you find that your work was well received? Did you enjoy any of your required quantitative subjects such as algebra or calculus?

The answers to questions such as these provide clues to skills and interests you bring to the employment market over and above the credential of your degree. In fact, it is not an overstatement to suggest that most employers who demand a college degree immediately look beyond that degree to you as a person and your own individual expression of what you like to do and think you can do for them, regardless of your major.

Collecting Job Titles

The world of employment is a big place, and even seasoned veterans of the job hunt can be surprised about what jobs are to be found in what organizations. You need to become a bit of an explorer and adventurer and be willing to try a variety of techniques to begin a list of possible occupations that might use your talents and education. Once you have a list of possibilities that you are interested in and qualified for, you can move on to find out what kinds of organizations have these job titles.

∙∙

Not every employer seeking to hire a publicist may be equally desirable to you. Some employment environments may be more attractive to you than others. A communications major considering public relations as a job could do that in a major corporation for either industrial or consumer goods, in a medical institution, a financial organization, or a small venture capital start-up company producing specialized computer software. Each of these environments presents a different culture with associated norms in the pace of work, the subject matter of interest, and the backgrounds of its employees. Although the job titles may be the same, not all locations may present the same fit for you.

If you majored in communications and enjoyed the in-class presentations you made as part of your degree and developed some good writing skills, you might naturally think law is a possibility for you. You're considering grad-

> uate school and a J.D. degree. But communications majors
> with these skills also become government managers, adver-
> tising executives, reporters, trainers, promotional cam-
> paign managers, and bank officers. Each of these job titles
> can also be found in a number of different settings.
>
> ······································

Take training, for example. Trainers write policy and procedural manu-
als and actively teach to assist all levels of employees in mastering various
tasks and work-related systems. Trainers exist in all large corporations, banks,
consumer goods manufacturers, medical diagnostic equipment firms, sales
organizations, and any organization that has processes or materials that need
to be presented to and learned by the staff.

In reading job descriptions or want ads for any of these positions, you
would find your four-year degree a "must." However, the academic major
might be less important than your own individual skills in critical thinking,
analysis, report writing, public presentations, and interpersonal communication. Even more important than thinking or knowing you have certain skills
are your ability to express those skills concretely and the examples you use
to illustrate them to an employer.

The best beginning to a job search is to create a list of job titles you might
want to pursue, learn more about the nature of the jobs behind those titles,
and then discover what kinds of employers hire for those positions. In the
following section we'll teach you how to build a job title directory to use in
your job search.

Developing a Job Title Directory That Works for You

A job title directory is simply a complete list of all the job titles you are interested in, are intrigued by, or think you are qualified for. After combining the
understanding gained through self-assessment with your own individual interests and the skills and talents you've acquired with your degree, you'll soon
start to read and recognize a number of occupational titles that seem right
for you. There are several resources you can use to develop your list, including computer searches, books, and want ads.

Computerized Interest Inventories. One way to begin your search is to identify a number of jobs that call for your degree and the particular skills and
interests you identified as part of the self-assessment process. There are
excellent interactive career-guidance programs on the market to help you
produce such selected lists of possible job titles. Most of these are available
at high schools and colleges and at some larger town and city libraries. Two

of the industry leaders are *CHOICES* and *DISCOVER*. Both allow you to enter interests, values, educational background, and other information to produce lists of possible occupations and industries. Each of the resources listed here will produce different job title lists. Some job titles will appear again and again, while others will be unique to a particular source. Investigate all of them!

Reference Sources. Books on the market that may be available through your local library or career counseling office also suggest various occupations related to specific majors. The following are only a few of the many good books on the market: *The College Board Guide to 150 Popular College Majors, College Majors and Careers: A Resource Guide for Effective Life Planning* both by Paul Phifer, and *Kaplan's What to Study: 101 Fields in a Flash.* All of these books list possible job titles within the academic major.

· ·

The *Occupational Thesaurus* is another good resource, which essentially lists job title possibilities under general categories. If you want to become an advertising executive and want to know more specific positions in the field, you can then go to the *Occupational Thesaurus*, which lists scores of jobs under that title. Under "Advertising," there are more than twenty associated job titles listed, including manufacturer's representative and customer relations specialist. If advertising was a suggested job title for you, this source adds some depth by suggesting a number of different occupations within that field.

· ·

Each job title deserves your consideration. Like removing the layers of an onion, the search for job titles can go on and on! As you spend time doing this activity, you are actually learning more about the value of your degree. What's important in your search at this point is not to become critical or selective but rather to develop as long a list of possibilities as you can. Every source used will help you add new and potentially exciting jobs to your growing list.

Want Ads. It has been well publicized that newspaper want ads represent only about 10 to 15 percent of the current job market. However, with the current high state of employment as this book goes to press, the percentage of jobs advertised in the newspapers and on-line is rising dramatically, so don't ignore this source.

If you are able to be mobile in your job search, you may want to search the classified sections of newspapers in other cities. This is now possible on-line. A good source for this search is the site called www.looksmart.com. Using the keywords *newspaper classifieds* will lead you to a site where you can search by state alphabetically. It's an excellent source for want ads.

Remember, because want ads are written for what an organization *hopes* to find, you don't have to meet absolutely every criterion. However, if certain requirements are stated as absolute minimums and you cannot meet them, it's best not to waste your time.

A recent examination of the *Boston Sunday Globe* (www.boston.com) reveals the following possible occupations for a liberal arts major with some computer skills and limited work experience. (This is only a partial list of what was available.)

- Admissions representative
- Salesperson
- Compliance director
- Assistant principal gifts writer
- Public relations officer

- Technical writer
- Personnel trainee
- G.E.D. examiner
- Direct mail researcher
- Associate publicist

After performing this exercise for a few Sundays, you'll find you have collected a new library of job titles.

The Sunday want ads exercise is important because these jobs are out in the marketplace. They truly exist, and people with your qualifications are being sought to apply. What's more, many of these advertisements describe the duties and responsibilities of the job advertised and give you a beginning sense of the challenges and opportunities such a position presents. Some will indicate salary, and that will be helpful as well. This information will better define the jobs for you and provide some good material for possible interviews in that field.

Exploring Job Descriptions

Once you've arrived at a solid list of possible job titles that interest you and for which you believe you are somewhat qualified, it's a good idea to do some research on each of these jobs. The preeminent source for such job information is the *Dictionary of Occupational Titles*, or *DOT* (www.wave.net /upg/immigration/dot_index.html). This directory lists every conceivable job and provides excellent up-to-date information on duties and responsibilities, interactions with associates, and day-to-day assignments and tasks. These descriptions provide a thorough job analysis, but they do not consider the possible employers or the environments in which a job may be performed. So, although a position as public relations officer may be well defined in terms of duties and responsibilities, it does not explain the differences in doing public relations work in a college or a hospital or a factory or a bank. You will need to look somewhere else for work settings.

Learning More About Possible Work Settings

After reading some job descriptions, you may choose to edit and revise your list of job titles once again, discarding those you feel are not suitable and keeping those that continue to hold your interest. Or you may wish to keep your list intact and see where these jobs may be located. For example, if you are interested in public relations and you appear to have those skills and the requisite education, you'll want to know what organizations do public relations. How can you find that out? How much income does someone in public relations make a year and what is the employment potential for the field of public relations?

To answer these and many other questions about your list of job titles, we recommend you try any of the following resources: *Careers Encyclopedia;* a career information center site such as that provided by the American Marketing Association at www.amaboston.org/jobs.htm; *College to Career: The Guide to Job Opportunities;* and the *Occupational Outlook Handbook* (http://stats.bls.gov/ocohome.htm). Each of these resources, in a different way, will help to put the job titles you have selected into an employer context. Perhaps the most extensive discussion is found in the *Occupational Outlook Handbook,* which gives a thorough presentation of the nature of the work, the working conditions, employment statistics, training, other qualifications, and advancement possibilities as well as job outlook and earnings. Related occupations are also detailed, and a select bibliography is provided to help you find additional information.

Continuing with our public relations example, your search through these reference materials would teach you that the public relations jobs you find attractive are available in larger hospitals, financial institutions, most corporations (both consumer goods and industrial goods), media organizations, and colleges and universities.

Networking to Get the Complete Story

You now have not only a list of job titles but also, for each of these job titles, a description of the work involved and a general list of possible employment settings in which to work. You'll want to do some reading and keep talking to friends, colleagues, teachers, and others about the possibilities. Don't neglect to ask if the career office at your college maintains some kind of alumni network. Often such alumni networks will connect you with another graduate from the college who is working in the job title or industry you are seeking information about. These career networkers offer what assistance they can. For some it is a full day "shadowing" the alumnus as he or she goes about the job. Others offer partial-day visits, tours, informational interviews, resume reviews, job postings, or, if distance prevents a visit, telephone interviews. As fellow graduates, they'll be frank and informative about their own jobs and prospects in their field.

Take them up on their offer and continue to learn all you can about your own personal list of job titles, descriptions, and employment settings. You'll probably continue to edit and refine this list as you learn more about the realities of the job, the possible salary, advancement opportunities, and supply and demand statistics.

In the next section we'll describe how to find the specific organizations that represent these industries and employers so that you can begin to make contact.

WHERE ARE THESE JOBS, ANYWAY?

Having a list of job titles that you've designed around your own career interests and skills is an excellent beginning. It means you've really thought about who you are and what you are presenting to the employment market. It has caused you to think seriously about the most appealing environments to work in, and you have identified some employer types that represent these environments.

The research and the thinking that you've done thus far will be used again and again. They will be helpful in writing your resume and cover letters, in talking about yourself on the telephone to prospective employers, and in answering interview questions.

Now is a good time to begin to narrow the field of job titles and employment sites down to some specific employers to initiate the employment contact.

Finding Out Which Employers Hire People Like You

This section will provide tips, techniques, and specific resources for developing an actual list of specific employers that can be used to make contacts. It is only an outline that you must be prepared to tailor to your own particular needs and according to what you bring to the job search. Once again, it is important to communicate with others along the way exactly what you're looking for and what your goals are for the research you're doing. Librarians, employers, career counselors, friends, friends of friends, business contacts, and bookstore staff will all have helpful information on geographically specific and new resources to aid you in locating employers who'll hire you.

Identifying Information Resources

Your interview wardrobe and your new resume might have put a dent in your wallet, but the resources you'll need to pursue your job search are available for free (although you may choose to copy materials on a machine instead of taking notes by hand). The categories of information detailed here are not hard to find and are yours for the browsing.

Numerous resources described in this section will help you identify actual employers. Use all of them or any others that you identify as available in your geographic area. As you become experienced in this process, you'll quickly figure out which information sources are helpful and which are not. If you live in a rural area, a well-planned day trip to a major city that includes a college career office, a large college or city library, state and federal employment centers, a chamber of commerce office, and a well-stocked bookstore can produce valuable results.

There are many excellent resources available to help you identify actual job sites. They are categorized into employer directories (usually indexed by product lines and geographic location), geographically based directories (designed to highlight particular cities, regions, or states), career-specific directories (e.g., *Sports MarketPlace*, which lists tens of thousands of firms involved with sports), periodicals and newspapers, targeted job posting publications, and videos. This is by no means meant to be a complete treatment of resources but rather a starting point for identifying useful resources.

Working from the more general references to highly specific resources, we provide a basic list to help you begin your search. Many of these you'll find easily available. In some cases reference librarians and others will suggest even better materials for your particular situation. Start to create your own customized bibliography of job search references. Use copying services to save time and to allow you to carry away information about organizations' missions, locations, company officers, phone numbers, and addresses.

Geographically Based Directories. The Job Bank series published by Bob Adams, Inc. (www.aip.com) contains detailed entries on each area's major employers, including business activity, address, phone number, and hiring contact name. Many listings specify educational backgrounds being sought in potential employees. Each volume contains a solid discussion of each city's or state's major employment sectors. Organizations are also indexed by industry. Job Bank volumes are available for the following places: Atlanta,

Boston, Chicago, Dallas–Ft. Worth, Denver, Detroit, Florida, Houston, Los Angeles, Minneapolis, New York, Ohio, Philadelphia, San Francisco, Seattle, St. Louis, Washington, D.C., and other cities throughout the Northwest.

National Job Bank (www.careercity.com) lists employers in every state, along with contact names and commonly hired job categories. Included are many small companies often overlooked by other directories. Companies are also indexed by industry. This publication provides information on educational backgrounds sought and lists company benefits.

Periodicals and Newspapers. Several sources are available to help you locate which journals or magazines carry job advertisements in your field. Other resources help you identify opportunities in other parts of the country.

■ *www.looksmart.com*
  If you want to search the classified sections of newspapers in other cities, a good source is this site. Using the keyword *newspaper classifieds* will lead you to where you can search alphabetically by state.

■ *www.careerpath.com*
  Connects to classified job ads from newspapers around the country. Select the job title and then select the state or region of the state.

Targeted Job Posting Publications. Although the resources that follow are national in scope, they are either targeted to one medium of contact (telephone), focused on specific types of jobs, or less comprehensive than the sources previously listed.

■ *Job Hotlines USA* (www.careers.org/topic/01_002.html)
  Pinpoints more than 1,000 hard-to-find telephone numbers for companies and government agencies that use prerecorded job messages and listings. Very few of the telephone numbers listed are toll-free, and sometimes recordings are long, so—callers, beware!

■ *The Job Hunter* (www.jobhunter.com)
  A national biweekly newspaper listing business, arts, media, government, human services, health, community-related, and student services job openings.

■ *Current Jobs for Graduates* (www.graduatejobs.com)
  A national employment listing for liberal arts professions, including editorial positions, management opportunities, museum work, teaching, and nonprofit work.

■ *Environmental Opportunities* (www.ecojobs.com)
  Serves environmental job interests nationwide by listing

administrative, marketing, and human resources positions along with education-related jobs and positions directly related to a degree in an environmental field.

■ *Y National Vacancy List*
(www.ymcahrm.ns.ca/employed/jobleads.html) Shows YMCA professional vacancies, including development, administration, programming, membership, and recreation postings.

■ *ARTSearch*
A national employment service bulletin for the arts, including administration, managerial, marketing, and financial management jobs.

■ *Community Jobs*
An employment newspaper for the nonprofit sector that provides a variety of listings, including project manager, canvas director, government relations specialist, community organizer, and program instructor.

■ *College Placement Council Annual: A Guide to Employment Opportunities for College Graduates*
An annual guide containing solid job-hunting information and, more important, displaying ads from large corporations actively seeking recent college graduates in all majors. Company profiles provide brief descriptions and available employment opportunities. Contact names and addresses are given. Profiles are indexed by organization name, geographic location, and occupation.

Videos. You may be one of the many job seekers who likes to get information via a medium other than paper. Many career libraries, public libraries, and career centers in libraries carry an assortment of videos that will help you learn new techniques and get information helpful in the job search.

Locating Information Resources

Throughout these introductory chapters, we have continually referred you to various websites for information on everything from job listings to career information. These same resources remain our best advice for your general research on career information. Using the Web gives you a mobility at your computer that you don't enjoy if you rely solely on books or newspapers or printed journals. Moreover, material on the Web, if the site is maintained, can be up-to-date, which may be crucial if you are looking at a cutting-edge career, in which technology changes almost daily. Federal government sites offer the option in some cases of downloading application materials, and many will accept your resume on-line.

You'll eventually identify the information resources that work best for you, but make certain you've covered the full range of resources before you begin to rely on a smaller list. Here's a short list of informational sites that many job seekers find helpful:

- Public and college libraries

- College career centers

- Bookstores

- Internet

- Local and state government personnel offices

Each one of these sites offers a collection of resources that will help you get the information you need.

As you meet and talk with service professionals at all these sites, be sure to let them know what you're doing. Inform them of your job search, what you've already accomplished, and what you're looking for. The more people who know you're job seeking, the greater the possibility that someone will have information or know someone who can help you along your way.

Public and College Libraries. Large city libraries, college and university libraries, and even well-supported town library collections contain a variety of resources to help you conduct a job search. It is not uncommon for libraries to have separate "vocational choices" sections with books, tapes, computer terminals, and associated materials relating to job search and selection. Some are now even making resume-creation software available for use by patrons.

Some of the publications we name throughout this book are expensive reference items that are rarely purchased by individuals. In addition, libraries carry a wide range of newspapers and telephone yellow pages as well as the usual array of books. If resources are not immediately available, many libraries have loan arrangements with other facilities and can make information available to you relatively quickly.

Take advantage not only of the reference collections but also of the skilled and informed staff. Let them know exactly what you are looking for, and they'll have their own suggestions. You'll be visiting the library frequently, and the reference staff will soon come to know who you are and what you're working on. They'll be part of your job search network!

College Career Centers. Career libraries, which are found in career centers at colleges and universities and sometimes within large public libraries, contain a unique blend of the job search resources housed in other settings. In addition, career libraries often purchase a number of job listing publications, each of which targets a specific industry or type of job. You may find job listings specifically for entry-level positions for your major. Ask about job posting newsletters or newspapers focused on careers in the area that most interests you. Each center will be unique, but you are certain to discover some good sources of jobs.

Most college career libraries now hold growing collections of video material on specific industries and on aspects of your job search process, including dress and appearance, how to manage the luncheon or dinner interview, how to be effective at a job fair, and many other titles. Some larger corporations produce handsome video materials detailing the variety of career paths and opportunities available in their organizations.

Some career libraries also house computer-based career planning and information systems. These interactive computer programs help you to clarify your values and interests and will combine them with your education to provide possible job titles and industry locations. Some even contain extensive lists of graduate school programs.

One specific kind of service a career library will be able to direct you to is computerized job search services. These services, of which there are many, are run by private companies, individual colleges, or consortiums of colleges. They attempt to match qualified job candidates with potential employers. The candidate submits a resume (or an application) to the service. This information (which can be categorized into hundreds of separate fields of data) is entered into a computer database. Your information is then compared with the information from employers about what they desire in a prospective employee. If there is a match between what they want and what you have indicated you can offer, the job search service or the employer will contact you directly to continue the process.

Computerized job search services can complement an otherwise complete job search program. They are *not*, however, a substitute for the kinds of activities described in this book. They are essentially passive operations that are random in nature. If you have not listed skills, abilities, traits, experiences, or education *exactly* as an employer has listed its needs, there is simply no match.

Consult with the staff members at the career libraries you use. These professionals have been specifically trained to meet the unique needs you present. Often you can just drop in and receive help with general questions, or you may want to set up an appointment to speak one-on-one with a career counselor to gain special assistance.

Every career library is different in size and content, but each can provide valuable information for the job search. Some may even provide limited counseling. If you have not visited the career library at your college or alma mater, call and ask if these collections are still available for your use. Be sure to ask about other services that you can use as well.

If you are not near your own college as you work on your job search, call the career office and inquire about reciprocal agreements with other colleges that are closer to where you live. Very often, your own alma mater can arrange for you to use a limited menu of services at another school. This typically would include access to a career library and job posting information and might include limited counseling.

Bookstores. Any well-stocked bookstore will carry some job search books that are worth buying. Some major stores will even have an extensive section devoted to materials, including excellent videos, related to the job search process. You will also find copies of local newspapers and business magazines. The one advantage that is provided by resources purchased at a bookstore is that you can read and work with the information in the comfort of your own home and do not have to conform to the hours of operation of a library, which can present real difficulties if you are working full-time as you seek employment. A few minutes spent browsing in a bookstore might be a beneficial break from your job search activities and turn up valuable resources.

Internet. There's no doubt about it, the Web is a job hunter's best friend. But the Web can also be an overwhelmingly abundant source of information—so much information that it becomes difficult to identify what's important and what is not. A simple search under the phrase *communications* can bring up sites that will be very meaningful for you and sites whose information is trivial and irrelevant to your job search. You need a strategy to master the Web, just as we advise a strategy to master the job search. Here are some suggestions:

1. Thoroughly utilize the websites identified throughout this guide. They've been chosen with you in mind, and many of them will be very helpful to you.

2. Begin to build your own portfolio of websites on your computer. Use the "bookmarking" function on your Web browser to build a series of bookmark folders for individual categories of good websites. You may have a folder for "entry-level job ad" sites and another folder for

"professional associations," and so on. Start your folders with the sites in this book that seem most helpful to you.

3. Visit your college career center (or ask for reciprocity consideration at a local college) and your nearby local and/or state and university libraries. All of these places have staff who are skilled researchers and can help you locate and identify more sites that are more closely targeted to your growing sense of job direction.

4. Use the E-mail function or Webmaster address that you'll find on many sites. Some sites encourage questions via E-mail. We have found that the response time to E-mail questions for website mailboxes can vary considerably, but more often than not, replies are quite prompt. Sometimes a website will list the E-mail of the "Webmaster" or "Webguru," and we have contacted those individuals with good success as well. So, if you have a question about a website, use these options to get satisfaction.

Local and State Government Personnel Offices. You'll learn that it's most efficient to establish a routine for checking job postings. Searching for a job is a full-time job (or should be!), and you don't want to waste time or feel that you're going around in circles. So, establish a routine by which each week, on the most appropriate day, you check out that day's resources. For example, if you live in a midsize city with a daily paper, you'll probably give the want ads a once-over every morning so that you can act immediately on any good job opening.

The same strategy applies to your local and state government personnel offices. Find out when and how they post jobs, and put those offices on your weekly checklist, so that you don't miss any reasonable openings. Your local municipality's personnel office may simply use a bulletin board in the town hall or a clipboard on a counter in the office. Make these stops part of your weekly routine, and you'll find that people begin to recognize you and become aware of your job search, which could prove to be very helpful. Most local governmental units are required to post jobs in public places for a stated period before the hiring process begins. It should be easy to find out where and how they do this. Keep a close eye on those sites.

State personnel offices are larger, less casual operations, but the principles are the same. State jobs are advertised, and the office can tell you what advertising mechanisms they use—which newspapers, what websites, and when jobs are posted. The personnel offices themselves are worth a visit, if you are close enough. In addition to all the current job postings, many state personnel offices have "spec sheets," which are detailed job specifications of all the positions they are apt to advertise. You could pick up a spec sheet for every job related to your area of interest and keep them in a file for later reference when such a job is advertised.

Many state personnel offices also publish a weekly or biweekly "open recruitment" listing of career opportunities that have not yet been filled. These listings are categorized by job title as well as by branch of government, and often by whether a test is needed to qualify for the position or not. An increasing number of state personnel or human resources offices are on-line and offer many services on the Web. A fine general website that can help you locate your state personnel office is www.piperinfo.com/state/index.cfm. While each state's site is different, you can count on access to the state human resources office and sometimes even the human resources offices of many of the state's larger cities. For example, the State of Connecticut lists an additional twenty-seven city sites that each have human resources departmental listings. So, you could search the State of Connecticut Human Resource Office and then jump to the City of Stamford and review city jobs on its site.

CHAPTER FOUR

NETWORKING

Networking is the process of deliberately establishing relationships to get career-related information or to alert potential employers that you are available for work. Networking is critically important to today's job seeker for two reasons: it will help you get the information you need, and it can help you find out about *all* of the available jobs.

GETTING THE INFORMATION YOU NEED

Networkers will review your resume and give you feedback on its effectiveness. They will talk about the job you are looking for and give you a candid appraisal of how they see your strengths and weaknesses. If they have a good sense of the industry or the employment sector for that job, you'll get their feelings on future trends in the industry as well. Some networkers will be very forthcoming about salaries, job-hunting techniques, and suggestions for your job search strategy. Many have been known to place calls right from the interview desk to friends and associates who might be interested in you. Each networker will make his or her own contribution, and each will be valuable.

Because organizations must evolve to adapt to current global market needs, the information provided by decision makers within various organizations will be critical to your success as a new job market entrant. For example, you might learn about the concept of virtual organizations from a networker. Virtual organizations coordinate economic activity to deliver value to customers by using resources outside the traditional boundaries of the organization. This concept is being discussed and implemented by chief executive officers of many organizations, including Ford Motor, Dell, and IBM.

Networking can help you find out about this and other trends currently affecting the industries under your consideration.

FINDING OUT ABOUT ALL OF THE AVAILABLE JOBS

Not every job that is available at this very moment is advertised for potential applicants to see. This is called the *hidden job market.* Only 15 to 20 percent of all jobs are formally advertised, which means that 80 to 85 percent of available jobs do not appear in published channels. Networking will help you become more knowledgeable about all the employment opportunities available during your job search period.

Although someone you might talk to today doesn't know of any openings within his or her organization, tomorrow or next week or next month an opening may occur. If you've taken the time to show an interest in and knowledge of their organization, if you've shown the company representative how you can help achieve organizational goals and that you can fit into the organization, you'll be one of the first candidates considered for the position.

NETWORKING: A PROACTIVE APPROACH

Networking is a proactive rather than a reactive approach. You, as a job seeker, are expected to initiate a certain level of activity on your own behalf; you cannot afford to simply respond to jobs listed in the newspaper. Being proactive means building a network of contacts that includes informed and interested decision makers who will provide you with up-to-date knowledge of the current job market and increase your chances of finding out about employment opportunities appropriate for your interests, experience, and level of education.

An old axiom of networking says, "You are only two phone calls away from the information you need." In other words, by talking to enough people, you will quickly come across someone who can offer you help. Start with your professors. Each of them probably has a wide circle of contacts. In their work and travel they might have met someone who can help you or direct you to someone who can.

CONTROL AND THE NETWORKING PROCESS

In deliberately establishing relationships, the process of networking begins with you in control—*you* are contacting specific individuals. As your network expands and you establish a set of professional relationships, your search for information or jobs will begin to move outside of your total control. A part of the networking process involves others assisting you by gathering information for you or recommending you as a possible job candidate. As additional people become a part of your networking system, you will have less knowledge about activities undertaken on your behalf; you will undoubtedly be contacted by individuals whom you did not initially approach. If you want to function effectively in surprise situations, you must be prepared at all times to talk with strangers about the informational or employment needs that motivated you to become involved in the networking process.

PREPARING TO NETWORK

In deliberately establishing relationships, maximize your efforts by organizing your approach. Five specific areas in which you can organize your efforts include reviewing your self-assessment, reviewing your research on job sites and organizations, deciding who it is you want to talk to, keeping track of all your efforts, and creating your self-promotion tools.

Review Your Self-Assessment

Your self-assessment is as important a tool in preparing to network as it has been in other aspects of your job search. You have carefully evaluated your personal traits, personal values, economic needs, longer-term goals, skill base, preferred skills, and underdeveloped skills. During the networking process you will be called upon to communicate what you know about yourself and relate it to the information or job you seek. Be sure to review the exercises that you completed in the self-assessment section of this book in preparation for networking. We've explained that you need to assess what skills you have acquired from your major that are of general value to an employer and to be ready to express those in ways employers can appreciate as useful in their own organizations.

Review Research on Job Sites and Organizations

In addition, individuals assisting you will expect that you'll have at least some background information on the occupation or industry of interest to you. Refer to the appropriate sections of this book and other relevant publications to acquire the background information necessary for effective networking. They'll explain how to identify not only the job titles that might be of interest to you but also what kinds of organizations employ people to do that job. You will develop some sense of working conditions and expectations about duties and responsibilities—all of which will be of help in your networking interviews.

Decide Who It Is You Want to Talk To

Networking cannot begin until you decide whom it is that you want to talk to and, in general, what type of information you hope to gain from your contacts. Once you know this, it's time to begin developing a list of contacts. Five useful sources for locating contacts are described here.

College Alumni Network. Most colleges and universities have created a formal network of alumni and friends of the institution who are particularly interested in helping currently enrolled students and graduates of their alma mater gain employment-related information.

· ·

Because communications is such a flexible degree program, you'll find an abundance of communications graduates spanning the full spectrum of possible employment. Just the diversity alone, as evidenced by such an alumni list, should be encouraging and informative to the communications graduate. Among such a diversified group, there are likely to be scores you would enjoy talking with an perhaps could meet.

· ·

It is usually a simple process to make use of an alumni network. Visit your college's website and locate the alumni office and/or your career center. Either or both sites will have information about your school's alumni network. You'll be provided with information on shadowing experiences, geographic information, or those alumni offering job referrals. If you don't find what you're looking for, don't hesitate to phone or E-mail your career center and ask what they can do to help you connect with an alum.

Alumni networkers may provide some combination of the following services: day-long shadowing experiences, telephone interviews, in-person interviews, information on relocating to given geographic areas, internship information, suggestions on graduate school study, and job vacancy notices.

· ·

What a valuable experience! Perhaps you are interested in working in law but don't think your research capabilities are up to the requirements of the profession. Spending a day with an attorney alumnus, asking lots of questions about the role of research in his or her job, and observing firsthand how much and what kind of research is going on will be a far better decision criterion for you than any reading on the subject could possibly provide.

In addition to your own observations, the alumnus will have his or her own perspective on the importance of research to a law career and which branches emphasize research and which may not. The law professional will give you realistic and honest feedback on your job search.

Present and Former Supervisors. If you believe you are on good terms with present or former job supervisors, they may be an excellent resource for providing information or directing you to appropriate resources that would have information related to your current interests and needs. Additionally, these supervisors probably belong to professional organizations that they might be willing to utilize to get information for you.

If, for example, you are interested in working with promotional campaigns for a service organization and you were currently working as an assistant in a local florist shop, talk with your supervisor or the owner. He or she may belong to the chamber of commerce, whose director would have information on local organizations that are in need of promotional help. You would be able to obtain the names and telephone numbers of these people, thus enabling you to begin the networking process.

Employers in Your Area. Although you may be interested in working in a geographic location different from the one where you currently reside, don't overlook the value of the knowledge and contacts those around you are able to provide. Use the local telephone directory and newspaper to identify the types of organizations you are thinking of working for or professionals who have the kinds of jobs you are interested in. Recently, a call made to a local hospital's financial administrator for information on working in health-care financial administration yielded more pertinent information on training seminars, regional professional organizations, and potential employment sites than a national organization was willing to provide.

Employers in Geographic Areas Where You Hope to Work. If you are thinking about relocating, identifying prospective employers or informational contacts in the new location will be critical to your success. Here are some tips for on-line searching. First, use a "metasearch" engine to get the most out of your search. Metasearch engines combine several engines into one powerful tool. We frequently use www.dogpile.com and www.metasearch.com for this purpose. Try using the city and state as your keywords in a search. *New Haven, Connecticut* will bring you to the city's website with links to the chamber of commerce, member businesses, and other valuable resources. By using www.looksmart.com you can locate newspapers in any area, and they, too, can provide valuable insight before you relocate. Of course, both dogpile and metasearch can lead you to yellow and white page directories in areas you are considering.

Professional Associations and Organizations. Professional associations and organizations can provide valuable information in several areas: career paths that you might not have considered, qualifications relating to those career choices, publications that list current job openings, and workshops or seminars that will enhance your professional knowledge and skills. They can also be excellent sources for background information on given industries: their health, current problems, and future challenges.

There are several excellent resources available to help you locate professional associations and organizations that would have information to meet your needs. Two especially useful publications are the *Encyclopedia of Associations* and *National Trade and Professional Associations of the United States.*

Keep Track of All Your Efforts

It can be difficult, almost impossible, to remember all the details related to each contact you make during the networking process, so you will want to develop a record-keeping system that works for you. Formalize this process by using your computer to keep a record of the people and organizations you want to contact. You can simply record the contact's name, address, and telephone number, and what information you hope to gain. Each entry might look something like this:

Contact Name	Address	Phone #	Purpose
Mr. Lee Perkins	13 Muromachi	73-8906	Local market
Osaka Branch	Osaka-shi		information

You could record this as a simple Word document and you could still use the "Find" function if you were trying to locate some data and could only recall the firm's name or the contact's name. If you're comfortable with database management and you have some database software on your computer, then you can put information at your fingertips even if you have only the zip code! The point here is not technological sophistication but good record keeping.

Once you have created this initial list, it will be helpful to keep more detailed information as you begin to actually make the contacts. Using the Network Contact Record form in Exhibit 4.1 will help you keep good information on all your network contacts. They'll appreciate your recall of details of your meetings and conversations, and the information will help you to focus your networking efforts.

Exhibit 4.1

NETWORK CONTACT RECORD

Name: (Be certain your spelling is correct.)

Title: (Pick up a business card to be certain of the correct title.)

Employing organization: (Note any parent company or subsidiaries.)

Business mailing address: (This Is often different from the street address.)

Business E-mail address:

Business telephone number: (Include area code and alternative numbers.)

Business fax number:

Source for this contact: (Who referred you, and what is their relationship to

the contact?)

Date of call or letter: (Use plenty of space here to record multiple phone calls or

visits, other employees you may have met, names of

secretaries/receptionists, and so forth.)

Content of discussion: (Keep enough notes here to remind you of the substance of

your visits and telephone conversations in case some time

elapses between contacts.)

Follow-up necessary to continue working with this contact: (Your contact may request that you send him or her some materials or direct you to contact an associate. Note any such instructions or assignments in this space.)

Name of additional networker: (Here you would record the names and phone numbers of

Address: additional contacts met at this employer's site. Often you will be introduced to many people, some of whom may indicate

E-mail: a willingness to help in your job search.)

Phone: _____

Fax: _____

Name of additional networker: _____

Address: _____

E-mail: _____

Phone: _____

Fax: _____

Name of additional networker: _____

Address: _____

E-mail: _____

Phone: _____

Fax: _____

Date thank-you note written: (May help to date your next contact.)

Follow-up action taken: (Phone calls, visits, additional notes.)

Other miscellaneous notes: (Record any other additional interaction you think may be important to remember in working with this networking client. You will want this form in front of you when telephoning or just before and after a visit.)

Create Your Self-Promotion Tools

There are two types of promotional tools that are used in the networking process. The first is a resume and cover letter, and the second is a one-minute "infomercial," which may be given over the telephone or in person.

Techniques for writing an effective resume and cover letter are discussed in Chapter 2. Once you have reviewed that material and prepared these important documents, you will have created one of your self-promotion tools.

The one-minute infomercial will demand that you begin tying your interests, abilities, and skills to the people or organizations you want to network with. Think about your goal for making the contact to help you understand what you should say about yourself. You should be able to express yourself easily and convincingly. If, for example, you are contacting an alumnus of your institution to obtain the names of possible employment sites in a distant city, be prepared to discuss why you are interested in moving to that location, the types of jobs you are interested in, and the skills and abilities you possess that will make you a qualified candidate.

To create a meaningful one-minute infomercial, write it out, practice it as if it will be a spoken presentation, rewrite it, and practice it again if necessary until expressing yourself comes easily and is convincing.

Here's a simplified example of an infomercial for use over the telephone:

....

Hello, Mr. Johnson? My name is Susan Roberts. I am a recent graduate of State College, and I wish to enter the advertising field. I was a business communications major and feel confident that I have many of the skills I understand are valued in advertising, such as writing, creativity, speaking, and delivering effective presentations. What's more, I work well under pressure. I have read that can be a real advantage in your business!

Mr. Johnson, I'm calling you because I still need more information about the advertising field. I'm hoping you'll have the time to sit down with me for about half an hour and discuss your perspective on advertising careers. There are so many possible places to get into advertising, and I am seeking some advice on which of those settings might be the best bet for my particular combination of skills and experience.

Would you be willing to do that for me? I would greatly appreciate it. I'm available most mornings, if that's convenient for you.

....

It very well may happen that your employer contact wishes you to communicate by E-mail. The infomercial quoted above could easily be rewritten for an E-mail message. You should "cut and paste" your resume right into the E-mail text itself.

Other effective self-promotion tools include portfolios for those in the arts, writing professions, or teaching. Portfolios show examples of work, photographs of projects or classroom activities, or certificates and credentials that are job related. There may not be an opportunity to use the portfolio during an interview, and it is not something that should be left with the organization. It is designed to be explained and displayed by the creator. However, during some networking meetings, there may be an opportunity to illustrate a point or strengthen a qualification by exhibiting the portfolio.

BEGINNING THE NETWORKING PROCESS

Set the Tone for Your Communications

It can be useful to establish "tone words" for any communications you embark upon. Before making your first telephone call or writing your first letter, decide what you want the person to think of you. If you are networking to try to obtain a job, your tone words might include descriptors such as *genuine, informed*, and *self-knowledgeable*. When you're trying to acquire information, your tone words may have a slightly different focus, such as *courteous, organized, focused*, and *well-spoken*. Use the tone words you establish for your contacts to guide you through the networking process.

Honestly Express Your Intentions

When contacting individuals, it is important to be honest about your reasons for making the contact. Establish your purpose in your own mind and be able and ready to articulate it concisely. Determine an initial agenda, whether it be informational questioning or self-promotion, present it to your contact, and be ready to respond immediately. If you don't adequately prepare before initiating your overture, you may find yourself at a disadvantage if you're asked to immediately begin your informational interview or self-promotion during the first phone conversation or visit.

Start Networking Within Your Circle of Confidence

Once you have organized your approach—by utilizing specific researching methods, creating a system for keeping track of the people you will contact, and developing effective self-promotion tools—you are ready to begin networking. The best way to begin networking is by talking with a group of people you trust and feel comfortable with. This group is usually made up of your family, friends, and career counselors. No matter who is in this inner circle, they will have a special interest in seeing you succeed in your job search. In addition, because they will be easy to talk to, you should try taking some risks in terms of practicing your information-seeking approach. Gain confidence in talking about the strengths you bring to an organization and the underdeveloped skills you feel hinder your candidacy. Be sure to review the section on self-assessment for tips on approaching each of these areas. Ask for critical but constructive feedback from the people in your circle of confidence on the letters you write and the one-minute infomercial you have developed. Evaluate whether you want to make the changes they suggest, then practice the changes on others within this circle.

Stretch the Boundaries of Your Networking Circle of Confidence

Once you have refined the promotional tools you will use to accomplish your networking goals, you will want to make additional contacts. Because you will not know most of these people, it will be a less comfortable activity to undertake. The practice that you gained with your inner circle of trusted friends should have prepared you to now move outside of that comfort zone.

It is said that any information a person needs is only two phone calls away, but the information cannot be gained until you (1) make a reasonable guess about who might have the information you need and (2) pick up the telephone to make the call. Using your network list that includes alumni, instructors, supervisors, employers, and associations, you can begin preparing your list of questions that will allow you to get the information you need. Review the question list that follows and then develop a list of your own.

Questions You Might Want to Ask

1. In the position you now hold, what do you do on a typical day?

2. What are the most interesting aspects of your job?

3. What part of your work do you consider dull or repetitious?

4. What were the jobs you had that led to your present position?

5. How long does it usually take to move from one step to the next in this career path?

6. What is the top position to which you can aspire in this career path?

7. What is the next step in *your* career path?

8. Are there positions in this field that are similar to your position?

9. What are the required qualifications and training for entry-level positions in this field?

10. Are there specific courses a student should take to be qualified to work in this field?

11. What are the entry-level jobs in this field?

12. What types of training are provided to persons entering this field?

13. What are the salary ranges your organization typically offers to entry-level candidates for positions in this field?

14. What special advice would you give a person entering this field?

15. Do you see this field as a growing one?

16. How do you see the content of the entry-level jobs in this field changing over the next two years?

17. What can I do to prepare myself for these changes?

18. What is the best way to obtain a position that will start me on a career in this field?

19. Do you have any information on job specifications and descriptions that I may have?

20. What related occupational fields would you suggest I explore?

21. How could I improve my resume for a career in this field?

22. Who else would you suggest I talk to, both in your organization and in other organizations?

Questions You Might Have to Answer

To communicate effectively, you must anticipate questions that will be asked of you by the networkers you contact. Review the following list and see if you can easily answer each of these questions. If you cannot, it may be time to revisit the self-assessment process.

1. Where did you get my name, or how did you find out about this organization?

2. What are your career goals?

3. What kind of job are you interested in?

4. What do you know about this organization and this industry?

5. How do you know you're prepared to undertake an entry-level position in this industry?

6. What course work have you done that is related to your career interests?

7. What are your short-term career goals?

8. What are your long-term career goals?

9. Do you plan to obtain additional formal education?

10. What contributions have you made to previous employers?

11. Which of your previous jobs have you enjoyed the most and why?

12. What are you particularly good at doing?

13. What shortcomings have you had to face in previous employment?

14. What are your three greatest strengths?

15. Describe how comfortable you feel with your communication style.

General Networking Tips

Make Every Contact Count. Setting the tone for each interaction is critical. Approaches that will help you communicate in an effective way include politeness, being appreciative of time provided to you, and being prepared and thorough. Remember, *everyone* within an organization has a circle of influence, so be prepared to interact effectively with each person you encounter in the networking process, including secretarial and support staff. Many information or job seekers have thwarted their own efforts by being rude to some individuals they encountered as they networked because they made the incorrect assumption that certain persons were unimportant.

Sometimes your contacts may be surprised at their ability to help you. After meeting and talking with you, they might think they have not offered much in the way of help. A day or two later, however, they may make a contact that would be useful to you and refer you to that person.

With Each Contact, Widen Your Circle of Networkers. Always leave an informational interview with the names of at least two more people who can help you get the information or job that you are seeking. Don't be shy about asking for additional contacts; networking is all about increasing the number of people you can interact with to achieve your goals.

Make Your Own Decisions. As you talk with different people and get answers to the questions you pose, you may hear conflicting information or get conflicting suggestions. Your job is to listen to these "experts" and decide what information and which suggestions will help you achieve *your* goals. Only implement those suggestions that you believe will work for you.

SHUTTING DOWN YOUR NETWORK

As you achieve the goals that motivated your networking activity—getting the information you need or the job you want—the time will come to inactivate all or parts of your network. As you do, be sure to tell your primary supporters about your change in status. Call or write to each one of them and give them as many details about your new status as you feel is necessary to maintain a positive relationship.

Because a network takes on a life of its own, activity undertaken on your behalf will continue even after you cease your efforts. As you get calls or are contacted in some fashion, be sure to inform these networkers about your change in status, and thank them for assistance they have provided.

Information on the latest employment trends indicates that workers will change jobs or careers several times in their lifetime. Networking, then, will be a critical aspect in the span of your professional life. If you carefully and thoughtfully conduct your networking activities during your job search, you will have a solid foundation of experience when you need to network the next time around.

CHAPTER FIVE

INTERVIEWING

C ertainly, there can be no one part of the job search process more fraught with anxiety and worry than the interview. Yet seasoned job seekers welcome the interview and will often say, "Just get me an interview and I'm on my way!" They understand that the interview is crucial to the hiring process and equally crucial for them, as job candidates, to have the opportunity of a personal dialogue to add to what the employer may already have learned from the resume, cover letter, and telephone conversations.

Believe it or not, the interview is to be welcomed, and even enjoyed! It is a perfect opportunity for you, the candidate, to sit down with an employer and express yourself and display who you are and what you want. Of course, it takes thought and planning and a little strategy; after all, it *is* a job interview! But it can be a positive, if not pleasant, experience and one you can look back on and feel confident about your performance and effort.

For many new job seekers, a job, any job, seems a wonderful thing. But seasoned interview veterans know that the job interview is an important step for both sides—the employer and the candidate—to see what each has to offer and whether there is going to be a "fit" of personalities, work styles, and attitudes. And it is this concept of balance in the interview, that both sides have important parts to play, that holds the key to success in mastering this aspect of the job search strategy.

Try to think of the interview as a conversation between two interested and equal partners. You both have important, even vital, information to deliver and to learn. Of course, there's no denying the employer has some leverage, especially in the initial interview for recruitment or any interview scheduled by the candidate and not the recruiter. That should not prevent the interviewee from seeking to play an equal part in what should be a fair exchange of information. Too often the untutored candidate allows the interview to become one-sided. The employer asks all the questions and the candidate simply responds. The ideal would be for two mutually interested parties to sit down and discuss possibilities for each. This is a conversation of significance, and it requires preparation, thought about the tone of the interview, and planning of the nature and details of the information to be exchanged.

PREPARING FOR THE INTERVIEW

The length of most initial interviews is about thirty minutes. Given the brevity, the information that is exchanged ought to be important. The candidate should be delivering material that the employer cannot discover on the resume, and in turn, the candidate should be learning things about the employer that he or she could not otherwise find out. After all, if you have only thirty minutes, why waste time on information that is already published? The information exchanged is more than just factual, and both sides will learn much from what they see of each other, as well. How the candidate looks, speaks, and acts are important to the employer. The employer's attention to the interview and awareness of the candidate's resume, the setting, and the quality of information presented are important to the candidate.

Just as the employer has every right to be disappointed when a prospect is late for the interview, looks unkempt, and seems ill-prepared to answer fairly standard questions, the candidate may be disappointed with an interviewer who isn't ready for the meeting, hasn't learned the basic resume facts, and is constantly interrupted by telephone calls. In either situation there's good reason to feel let down.

There are many elements to a successful interview, and some of them are not easy to describe or prepare for. Sometimes there is just a chemistry between interviewer and interviewee that brings out the best in both, and a good exchange takes place. But there is much the candidate can do to pave the way for success in terms of his or her resume, personal appearance, goals, and interview strategy—each of which we will discuss. However, none of this preparation is as important as the time and thought the candidate gives to personal self-assessment.

Self-Assessment

Neither a stunning resume nor an expensive, well-tailored suit can compensate for candidates who do not know what they want, where they are going, or why they are interviewing with a particular employer. Self-assessment, the process by which we begin to know and acknowledge our own particular blend of education, experiences, needs, and goals, is not something that can be sorted out the weekend before a major interview. Of all the elements of interview preparation, this one requires the longest lead time and cannot be faked.

Because the time allotted for most interviews is brief, it is all the more important for job candidates to understand and express succinctly why they are there and what they have to offer. This is not a time for undue modesty (or for braggadocio either); it is a time for a compelling, reasoned statement of why you feel that you and this employer might make a good match. It means you have to have thought about your skills, interests, and attributes; related those to your life experiences and your own history of challenges and opportunities; and determined what that indicates about your strengths, preferences, values, and areas needing further development.

A common complaint of employers is that many candidates didn't take advantage of the interview time; they didn't seem to know why they were there or what they wanted. When candidates are asked to talk about themselves and their work-related skills and attributes, employers don't want to be faced with shyness or embarrassed laughter; they need to know about you so they can make a fair determination of you and your competition. If you don't take advantage of the opportunity to make a case for your employability, you can be certain the person ahead of you has or the person after you will, and it will be on the strength of those impressions that the employer will hire.

If you need some assistance with self-assessment issues, refer to Chapter 1. Included are suggested exercises that can be done as needed, such as making up an experiential diary and extracting obvious strengths and weaknesses from past experiences. These simple assignments will help you look at past activities as collections of tasks with accompanying skills and responsibilities. Don't overlook your high school or college career office. Many offer personal counseling on self-assessment issues and may provide testing instruments such as the *Myers-Briggs Type Indicator* (*MBTI*), the *Harrington-O'Shea Career Decision-Making System* (*CDM*), the *Strong Interest Inventory* (*SII*), or any other of a wide selection of assessment tools that can help you clarify some of these issues prior to the interview stage of your job search.

The Resume

Resume preparation has been discussed in detail, and some basic examples of various types were provided. In this section we want to concentrate on how best to use your resume in the interview. In most cases the employer will have seen the resume prior to the interview, and, in fact, it may well have been the quality of that resume that secured the interview opportunity.

An interview is a conversation, however, and not an exercise in reading. So, if the employer hasn't seen your resume and you have brought it along to the interview, wait until asked or until the end of the interview to offer it. Otherwise, you may find yourself staring at the back of your resume and simply answering "yes" and "no" to a series of questions drawn from that document.

Sometimes an interviewer is not prepared and does not know or recall the contents of the resume and may use the resume to a greater or lesser degree as a "prompt" during the interview. It is for you to judge what that may indicate about the individual performing the interview or the employer. If your interviewer seems surprised by the scheduled meeting, relies on the resume to an inordinate degree, and seems otherwise unfamiliar with your background, this lack of preparation for the hiring process could well be a symptom of general management disorganization or may simply be the result of poor planning on the part of one individual. It is your responsibility as a potential employee to be aware of these signals and make your decisions accordingly.

· ·

In any event, it is perfectly acceptable for you to get the conversation back to a more interpersonal style by saying something such as, "Mr. Jones, you might be interested in some recent publishing experience I gained in an internship that is not detailed on my resume. May I tell you about it?" This can return the interview to two people talking to each other, not one reading and the other responding.

· ·

By all means, bring at least one copy of your resume to the interview. Occasionally, at the close of an interview, an interviewer will express an interest in circulating a resume to several departments, and you could then offer the copy you brought. Sometimes, an interview appointment provides an opportunity to meet others in the organization who may express an interest in you and your background, and it may be helpful to follow up with a copy of your resume. Our best advice, however, is to keep it out of sight until needed or requested.

Appearance

Although many of the absolute rules that once dominated the advice offered to job candidates about appearance have now been moderated significantly, conservative is still the watchword unless you are interviewing in a fashion-related industry. For men, conservative translates into a well-cut dark suit with appropriate tie, hosiery, and dress shirt. A wise strategy for the male job seeker looking for a good but not expensive suit would be to try the men's department of a major department store. They usually carry a good range of sizes, fabrics, and prices; offer professional sales help; provide free tailoring; and have associated departments for putting together a professional look.

For women, there is more latitude. Business suits are still popular, but they have become more feminine in color and styling with a variety of jacket and skirt lengths. In addition to suits, better-quality dresses are now worn in many environments and, with the correct accessories, can be most appropriate. Company literature, professional magazines, the business section of major newspapers, and television interviews can all give clues about what is being worn in different employer environments.

Both men and women need to pay attention to issues such as hair, jewelry, and makeup; these are often what separates the candidate in appearance from the professional workforce. It seems particularly difficult for the young job seeker to give up certain hairstyles, eyeglass fashions, and jewelry habits, yet those can be important to the employer who is concerned with your ability to successfully make the transition into the organization. Candidates often find the best strategy is to dress conservatively until they find employment. Once employed and familiar with the norms within your organization, you can begin to determine a look that you enjoy, works for you, and fits your organization.

Choose clothes that suit your body type, fit well, and flatter you. Feel good about the way you look! The interview day is not the best time for a new hairdo, a new pair of shoes, or any other change that will distract you or cause you to be self-conscious. Arrive a bit early to avoid being rushed, and ask the receptionist to direct you to a restroom for any last-minute adjustments of hair and clothes.

Employer Information

Whether your interview is for graduate school admission, an overseas corporate position, or a reporter position with a local newspaper, it is important to know something about the employer or the organization. Keeping in mind that the interview is relatively brief and that you will hopefully have other interviews with other organizations, it is important to keep your research in proportion. If secondary interviews are called for, you will have additional time to do further research. For the first interview, it is helpful to know the organization's mission, goals, size, scope of operations, and so forth. Your research may uncover recent areas of challenge or particular successes that may help to fuel the interview. Use the "What Do They Call the Job You Want?" section of Chapter 3, your library, and your career or guidance office to help you locate this information in the most efficient way possible. Don't be shy in asking advice of these counseling and guidance professionals on how best to spend your preparation time. With some practice, you'll soon learn how much information is enough and which kinds of information are most useful to you.

INTERVIEW CONTENT

We've already discussed how it can help to think of the interview as an important conversation—one that, as with any conversation, you want to find pleasant and interesting and to leave you with a good feeling. But because this conversation is especially important, the information that's exchanged is critical to its success. What do you want them to know about you? What do you need to know about them? What interview technique do you need to particularly pay attention to? How do you want to manage the close of the interview? What steps will follow in the hiring process?

Except for the professional interviewer, most of us find interviewing stressful and anxiety-provoking. Developing a strategy before you begin interviewing will help you relieve some stress and anxiety. One particular strategy that has worked for many and may work for you is interviewing by objective. Before you interview, write down three to five goals you would like to achieve for that interview. They may be technique goals: smile a little more, have a firmer handshake, be sure to ask about the next stage in the interview process before leaving. They may be content-oriented goals: find out about the company's current challenges and opportunities; be sure to speak of your recent research, writing experiences, or foreign travel. Whatever your goals, jot down a few of them as goals for each interview.

Most people find that in trying to achieve these few goals, their interviewing technique becomes more organized and focused. After the interview, the most common question friends and family ask is "How did it go?" With this technique, you have an indication of whether you met *your* goals for the meeting, not just some vague idea of how it went. Chances are, if you accomplished what you wanted to, it improved the quality of the entire interview. As you continue to interview, you will want to revise your goals to continue improving your interview skills.

Now, add to the concept of the significant conversation the idea of a beginning, a middle, and a closing and you will have two thoughts that will give your interview a distinctive character. Be sure to make your introduction warm and cordial. Say your full name (and if it's a difficult-to-pronounce name, help the interviewer to pronounce it) and make certain you know your interviewer's name and how to pronounce it. Most interviews begin with some "soft talk" about the weather, chat about the candidate's trip to the interview site, or national events. This is done as a courtesy to relax both you and the interviewer, to get you talking, and to generally try to defuse the atmosphere of excessive tension. Try to be yourself, engage in the conversation, and don't try to second-guess the interviewer. This is simply what it appears to be—casual conversation.

Once you and the interviewer move on to exchange more serious information in the middle part of the interview, the two most important concerns become your ability to handle challenging questions and your success at asking meaningful ones. Interviewer questions will probably fall into one of three categories: personal assessment and career direction, academic assessment, and knowledge of the employer. The following are some examples of questions in each category:

Personal Assessment and Career Direction

1. How would you describe yourself?

2. What motivates you to put forth your best effort?

3. In what kind of work environment are you most comfortable?

4. What do you consider to be your greatest strengths and weaknesses?

5. How well do you work under pressure?

6. What qualifications do you have that make you think you will be successful in this career?

7. Will you relocate? What do you feel would be the most difficult aspect of relocating?

8. Are you willing to travel?

9. Why should I hire you?

Academic Assessment

1. Why did you select your college or university?

2. What changes would you make at your alma mater?

3. What led you to choose your major?

4. What subjects did you like best and least? Why?

5. If you could, how would you plan your academic study differently? Why?

6. Describe your most rewarding college experience.

7. How has your college experience prepared you for this career?

8. Do you think that your grades are a good indication of your ability to succeed with this organization?

9. Do you have plans for continued study?

Knowledge of the Employer

1. If you were hiring a graduate of your school for this position, what qualities would you look for?

2. What do you think it takes to be successful in an organization like ours?

3. In what ways do you think you can make a contribution to our organization?

4. Why did you choose to seek a position with this organization?

The interviewer wants a response to each question but is also gauging your enthusiasm, preparedness, and willingness to communicate. In each response you should provide some information about yourself that can be related to the employer's needs. A common mistake is to give too much information. Answer each question completely, but be careful not to run on too long with extensive details or examples.

Questions About Underdeveloped Skills

Most employers interview people who have met some minimum criteria of education and experience. They interview candidates to see who they are, to learn what kind of personality they exhibit, and to get some sense of how this person might fit into the existing organization. It may be that you are asked about skills the employer hopes to find and that you have not documented. Maybe it's grant-writing experience, knowledge of the European political system, or a knowledge of the film world.

To questions about skills and experiences you don't have, answer honestly and forthrightly and try to offer some additional information about skills you do have. For example, perhaps the employer is disappointed you have no grant-writing experience. An honest answer may be as follows:

No, unfortunately, I was never in a position to acquire those skills. I do understand something of the complexities of the grant-writing process and feel confident that my attention to detail, careful reading skills, and strong writing would make grants a wonderful challenge in a new job. I think I could get up on the learning curve quickly.

The employer hears an honest admission of lack of experience but is reassured by some specific skill details that do relate to grant writing and a confident manner that suggests enthusiasm and interest in a challenge.

For many students, questions about their possible contribution to an employer's organization can prove challenging. Because your education has probably not included specific training for a job, you need to review your academic record and select capabilities you have developed in your major that an employer can appreciate. For example, perhaps you read well and can analyze and condense what you've read into smaller, more focused pieces. That could be valuable. Or maybe you did some serious research and you know you have valuable investigative skills. Your public speaking might be highly developed and you might use visual aids appropriately and effectively. Or maybe your skill at correspondence, memos, and messages is effective. Whatever it is, you must take it out of the academic context and put it into a new, employer-friendly context so your interviewer can best judge how you could help the organization.

Exhibiting knowledge of the organization will, without a doubt, show the interviewer that you are interested enough in the available position to have done some legwork in preparation for the interview. Remember, it is not necessary to know every detail of the organization's history but rather to have a general knowledge about why it is in business and how the industry is faring.

Sometime during the interview, generally after the midway point, you'll be asked if you have any questions for the interviewer. Your questions will tell the employer much about your attitude and your desire to understand the organization's expectations so you can compare it to your own strengths. The following are some selected questions you might want to ask:

1. What are the main responsibilities of the position?

2. What are the opportunities and challenges associated with this position?

3. Could you outline some possible career paths beginning with this position?

4. How regularly do performance evaluations occur?

5. What is the communication style of the organization? (meetings, memos, and so forth)

6. What would a typical day in this position be like for me?

7. What kinds of opportunities might exist for me to improve my professional skills within the organization?

8. What have been some of the interesting challenges and opportunities your organization has recently faced?

Most interviews draw to a natural closing point, so be careful not to prolong the discussion. At a signal from the interviewer, wind up your presentation, express your appreciation for the opportunity, and be sure to ask what the next stage in the process will be. When can you expect to hear from them? Will they be conducting second-tier interviews? If you are interested and haven't heard, would they mind a phone call? Be sure to collect a business card with the name and phone number of your interviewer. On your way out, you might have an opportunity to pick up organizational literature you haven't seen before.

With the right preparation—a thorough self-assessment, professional clothing, and employer information—you'll be able to set and achieve the goals you have established for the interview process.

CHAPTER SIX

NETWORKING OR INTERVIEW FOLLOW-UP

Quite often there is a considerable time lag between interviewing for a position and being hired or, in the case of the networker, between your phone call or letter to a possible contact and the opportunity of a meeting. This can be frustrating. "Why aren't they contacting me?" "I thought I'd get another interview, but no one has telephoned." "Am I out of the running?" You don't know what is happening.

CONSIDER THE DIFFERING PERSPECTIVES

Of course, there is another perspective—that of the networker or hiring organization. Organizations are complex, with multiple tasks that need to be accomplished each day. Hiring is a discrete activity that does not occur as frequently as other job assignments. The hiring process might have to take second place to other, more immediate organizational needs. Although it may be very important to you, and it is certainly ultimately significant to the employer, other issues such as fiscal management, planning and product development, employer vacation periods, or financial constraints may prevent an organization or individual within that organization from acting on your employment or your request for information as quickly as you or they would prefer.

USE YOUR COMMUNICATION SKILLS

Good communication is essential here to resolve any anxieties, and the responsibility is on you, the job or information seeker. Too many job seekers and networkers offer as an excuse that they don't want to "bother" the organization by writing letters or calling. Let us assure you here and now, once and for all, that if you are troubling an organization by over-communicating, someone will indicate that situation to you quite clearly. If not, you can only assume you are a worthwhile prospect and the employer appreciates being reminded of your availability and interest. Let's look at follow-up practices in the job interview process and the networking situation separately.

FOLLOWING UP ON THE EMPLOYMENT INTERVIEW

A brief thank-you note following an interview is an excellent and polite way to begin a series of follow-up communications with a potential employer with whom you have interviewed and want to remain in touch. It should be just that—a thank-you for a good meeting. If you failed to mention some fact or experience during your interview that you think might add to your candidacy, you may use this note to do that. However, this should be essentially a note whose overall tone is appreciative and, if appropriate, indicative of a continuing interest in pursuing any opportunity that may exist with that organization. It is one of the few pieces of business correspondence that may be handwritten, but always use plain, good-quality, standard-size paper.

If, however, at this point you are no longer interested in the employer, the thank-you note is an appropriate time to indicate that. You are under no obligation to identify any reason for not continuing to pursue employment with that organization, but if you are so inclined to indicate your professional reasons (pursuing other employers more akin to your interests, looking for greater income production than this employer can provide, a different geographic location), you certainly may. It should not be written with an eye to negotiation, for it will not be interpreted as such.

As part of your interview closing, you should have taken the initiative to establish lines of communication for continuing information about your candidacy. If you asked permission to telephone, wait a week following your thank-you note, then telephone your contact simply to inquire how things are progressing on your employment status. The feedback you receive here should be taken at face value. If your interviewer simply has no information, he or she will tell you so and indicate whether you should call again and when. Don't be discouraged if this should continue over some period of time.

If during this time something occurs that you think improves or changes your candidacy (some new qualification or experience you may have had), including any offers from other organizations, by all means telephone or write to inform the employer about this. In the case of an offer from a competing but less desirable or equally desirable organization, telephone your contact, explain what has happened, express your real interest in the organization, and inquire whether some determination on your employment might be made before you must respond to this other offer. An organization that is truly interested in you may be moved to make a decision about your candidacy. Equally possible is the scenario in which they are not yet ready to make a decision and so advise you to take the offer that has been presented. Again, you have no ethical alternative but to deal with the information presented in a straightforward manner.

When accepting other employment, be sure to contact any employers still actively considering you and inform them of your new job. Thank them graciously for their consideration. There are many other job seekers out there just like you who will benefit from having their candidacy improved when others bow out of the race. Who knows, you might at some future time have occasion to interact professionally with one of the organizations with which you sought employment. How embarrassing it would be to have someone remember you as the candidate who failed to notify them that you were taking a job elsewhere!

In all of your follow-up communications, keep good notes of whom you spoke with, when you called, and any instructions that were given about return communications. This will prevent any misunderstandings and provide you with good records of what has transpired.

FOLLOWING UP ON THE NETWORK CONTACT

Far more common than the forgotten follow-up after an interview is the situation where a good network contact is allowed to lapse. Good communications are the essence of a network, and follow-up is not so much a matter of courtesy here as it is a necessity. In networking for job information and contacts, you are the active network link. Without you, and without continual contact from you, there is no network. You and your need for employment are often the only shared elements among members of the network. Because network contacts were made regardless of the availability of any particular employment, it is incumbent upon the job seeker, if not simple common sense, to stay in regular communication with the network if you want to be considered for any future job opportunities.

This brings up the issue of responsibility, which is likewise very clear. The job seeker initiates network contacts and is responsible for maintaining those contacts; therefore, the entire responsibility for the network belongs with him or her. This becomes patently obvious if the network is left unattended. It very shortly falls out of existence because it cannot survive without careful attention by the networker.

You have many ways to keep the lines of communication open and to attempt to interest the network in you as a possible employee. You are limited only by your own enthusiasm for members of the network and your creativity. However, you as a networker are well advised to keep good records of whom you have met and contacted in each organization. Be sure to send thank-you notes to anyone who has spent any time with you, whether it was an E-mail message containing information or advice, a quick tour of a department, or a sit-down informational interview. All of these thank-you notes should, in addition to their ostensible reason, add some information about you and your particular combination of strengths and attributes.

You can contact your network at any time to convey continued interest, to comment on some recent article you came across concerning an organization, to add information about your training or changes in your qualifications, to ask advice or seek guidance in your job search, or to request referrals to other possible network opportunities. Sometimes just a simple note to network members reminding them of your job search, indicating that you have been using their advice, and noting that you are still actively pursuing leads and hope to continue to interact with them is enough to keep communications alive.

The Internet has opened up the world of networking. You may be able to find networkers who graduated from your high school or from the college you're attending, who live in a geographic region where you hope to work, or who are employed in a given industry. The Internet makes it easy to reach out to many people, but don't let this perceived ease lull you into complacency. Internet networking demands the same level of preparation as the more traditional forms of networking.

Because networks have been abused in the past, it's important that your conduct be above reproach. Networks are exploratory options; they are not backdoor access to employers. The network works best for someone who is exploring a new industry or making a transition into a new area of employment and who needs to find information or to alert people to his or her search activity. Always be candid and direct with contacts in expressing the purpose of your E-mail, call, or letter and your interest in their help or information about their organization. In follow-up contacts keep the tone professional and direct. Your honesty will be appreciated, and people will respond as best they can if your qualifications appear to meet their forthcoming needs. The network does not owe you anything, and that tone should be clear to each person you meet.

FEEDBACK FROM FOLLOW-UPS

A network contact may prove to be miscalculated. Perhaps you were referred to someone and it became clear that your goals and his or her particular needs did not make a good match. Or the network contact may simply not be in a position to provide you with the information you are seeking. Or in some unfortunate situations, the party may become annoyed by being contacted for this purpose. In such a situation, many job seekers simply say "Thank you" and move on.

If the contact is simply not the right connection, but the individual you are speaking with is not annoyed by the call, it might be a better tactic to express regret that the contact was misplaced and then tell the person what you are seeking and ask for his or her advice or possible suggestions as to a next step. The more people who are aware that you are seeking employment, the better your chances of connecting, and that is the purpose of a network. Most people in a profession have excellent knowledge of their field and varying amounts of expertise in areas tangent to their own. Use their expertise and seek some guidance before you dissolve the contact. You may be pleasantly surprised.

Occasionally, networkers will express the feeling that they have done as much as they can or provided all the information that is available to them. This may be a cue that they would like to be released from your network. Be alert to such attempts to terminate, graciously thank the individual by letter, and move on in your network development. A network is always changing, adding, and losing members, and you want the network to be composed only of those who are actively interested in supporting you.

A FINAL POINT ON NETWORKING FOR COMMUNICATIONS MAJORS

In any of the fields that a communications major might consider as a potential career path, networkers and interviewers will be evaluating all of your written and oral communications. As a communications major, this should be gratifying, but at the same time it emphasizes the importance of the quality of your interactions with people who are in a position to help you in your job search.

In your telephone communications, interview presentations, follow-up correspondence, and ability to deal with negative feedback, your warmth, style, and personality, as evidenced in your written and spoken use of English, will be part of the portfolio of impressions you create in those you meet along the way.

CHAPTER SEVEN

JOB OFFER CONSIDERATIONS

f or many recent college graduates, the thrill of their first job and, for some, the most substantial regular income they have ever earned seems an excess of good fortune coming at once. To question that first income or to be critical in any way of the conditions of employment at the time of the initial offer seems like looking a gift horse in the mouth. It doesn't seem to occur to many new hires even to attempt to negotiate any aspect of their first job. And, as many employers who deal with entry-level jobs for recent college graduates will readily confirm, the reality is that there simply isn't much movement in salary available to these new college recruits. The entry-level hire generally does not have an employment track record on a professional level to provide any leverage for negotiation. Real negotiations on salary, benefits, retirement provisions, and so forth come to those with significant employment records at higher income levels.

Of course, the job offer is more than just money. It can be composed of geographic assignment, duties and responsibilities, training, benefits, health and medical insurance, educational assistance, car allowance or company vehicle, and a host of other items. All of this is generally detailed in the formal letter that presents the final job offer. In most cases this is a follow-up to a personal phone call from the employer representative who has been principally responsible for your hiring process.

That initial telephone offer is certainly binding as a verbal agreement, but most firms follow up with a detailed letter outlining the most significant parts of your employment contract. You may, of course, choose to respond immediately at the time of the telephone offer (which would be considered a binding oral contract), but you will also be required to formally answer the letter of offer with a letter of acceptance, restating the salient elements of the employer's description of your position, salary, and benefits. This ensures that both parties are clear on the terms and conditions of employment and remuneration and any other outstanding aspects of the job offer.

IS THIS THE JOB YOU WANT?

Most new employees will respond affirmatively in writing, glad to be in the position to accept employment. If you've worked hard to get the offer and the job market is tight, other offers may not be in sight, so you will say, "Yes, I accept!" What is important here is that the job offer you accept be one that does fit your particular needs, values, and interests as you've outlined them in your self-assessment process. Moreover, it should be a job that will not only use your skills and education but also challenge you to develop new skills and talents.

Jobs are sometimes accepted too hastily, for the wrong reasons, and without proper scrutiny by the applicant. For example, an individual might readily accept a sales job only to find the continual rejection by potential clients unendurable. An office worker might realize within weeks the constraints of a desk job and yearn for more activity. Employment is an important part of our lives. It is, for most of our adult lives, our most continuous productive activity. We want to make good choices based on the right criteria.

If you have a low tolerance for risk, a job based on commission will certainly be very anxiety-provoking. If being near your family is important, issues of relocation could present a decision crisis for you. If you're an adventurous person, a job with frequent travel would provide needed excitement and be very desirable. The importance of income, the need to continue your education, your personal health situation—all of these have an impact on whether the job you are considering will ultimately meet your needs. Unless you've spent some time understanding and thinking about these issues, it will be difficult to evaluate offers you do receive.

More important, if you make a decision that you cannot tolerate and feel you must leave that job, you will then have both unemployment and self-esteem issues to contend with. These will combine to make the next job search tough going, indeed. So make your acceptance a carefully considered decision.

NEGOTIATING YOUR OFFER

It may be that there is some aspect of your job offer that is not particularly attractive to you. Perhaps there is no relocation allotment to help you move your possessions, and this presents some financial hardship for you. It may be that the health insurance is less than you had hoped. Your initial assignment may be different from what you expected, either in its location or in the duties and responsibilities that comprise it. Or it may simply be that the salary is less than you anticipated. Other considerations may be your official starting date of employment, vacation time, evening hours, dates of training programs or schools, and other concerns.

If you are considering not accepting the job because of some item or items in the job offer "package" that do not meet your needs, you should know that most employers emphatically wish that you would bring that issue to their attention. It may be that the employer can alter it to make the offer more agreeable for you. In some cases it cannot be changed. In any event the employer would generally like to have the opportunity to try to remedy a difficulty rather than risk losing a good potential employee over an issue that might have been resolved. After all, they have spent time and funds in securing your services, and they certainly deserve an opportunity to resolve any possible differences.

Honesty is the best approach in discussing any objections or uneasiness you might have over the employer's offer. Having received your formal offer in writing, contact your employer representative and indicate your particular dissatisfaction in a straightforward manner. For example, you might explain that while you are very interested in being employed by this organization, the salary (or any other benefit) is less than you have determined you require. State the terms you need, and listen to the response. You may be asked to put this in writing, or you may be asked to hold off until the firm can decide on a response. If you are dealing with a senior representative of the organization, one who has been involved in hiring for some time, you may get an immediate response or a solid indication of possible outcomes.

Perhaps the issue is one of relocation. Your initial assignment is in the Midwest, and because you had indicated a strong West Coast preference, you are surprised at the actual assignment. You might simply indicate that while you understand the need for the company to assign you based on its needs, you are disappointed and had hoped to be placed on the West Coast. You could inquire if that were still possible and, if not, would it be reasonable to expect a West Coast relocation in the future.

If your request is presented in a reasonable way, most employers will not see this as jeopardizing your offer. If they can agree to your proposal, they will. If not, they will simply tell you so, and you may choose to continue your candidacy with them or remove yourself from consideration. The choice will be up to you.

Some firms will adjust benefits within their parameters to meet the candidate's need if at all possible. If a candidate requires a relocation cost allowance, he or she may be asked to forego tuition benefits for the first year to accomplish this adjustment. An increase in life insurance may be adjusted by some other benefit trade-off; perhaps a family dental plan is not needed. In these decisions you are called upon, sometimes under time pressure, to know how you value these issues and how important each is to you.

Many employers find they are more comfortable negotiating for candidates who have unique qualifications or who bring especially needed expertise to the organization. Employers hiring large numbers of entry-level college graduates may be far more reluctant to accommodate any changes in offer conditions. They are well supplied with candidates with similar education and experience so that if rejected by one candidate, they can draw new candidates from an ample labor pool.

COMPARING OFFERS

The condition of the economy, the job seekers' academic major and particular geographic job market, and individual needs and demands for certain employment conditions may not provide more than one job offer at a time. Some job seekers may feel that no reasonable offer should go unaccepted for the simple fear there won't be another.

In a tough job market, or if the job you seek is not widely available, or when your job search goes on too long and becomes difficult to sustain financially and emotionally, it may be necessary to accept an inferior offer. The alternative is continued unemployment. Even here, when you feel you don't have a choice, you can at least understand that in accepting this particular offer, there may be limitations and conditions you don't appreciate. At the time of acceptance, there were no other alternatives, but you can begin to use that position to gain the experience and talent to move toward a more attractive position.

Sometimes, however, more than one offer is received, and the candidate has the luxury of choice. If the job seeker knows what he or she wants and has done the necessary self-assessment honestly and thoroughly, it may be clear that one of the offers conforms more closely to those expressed wants and needs.

However, if, as so often happens, the offers are similar in terms of conditions and salary, the question then becomes which organization might provide the necessary climate, opportunities, and advantages for your professional development and growth. This is the time when solid employer research and astute questioning during the interviews really pays off. How much did you learn about the employer through your own research and skillful questioning? When the interviewer asked during the interview "Do you have any questions?" did you ask the kinds of questions that would help resolve a choice between one organization and another? Just as an employer must decide among numerous applicants, so must the applicant learn to assess the potential employer. Both are partners in the job search.

RENEGING ON AN OFFER

An especially disturbing occurrence for employers and career counseling professionals is when a job seeker formally (either orally or by written contract) accepts employment with one organization and later reneges on the agreement and goes with another employer.

There are all kinds of rationalizations offered for this unethical behavior. None of them satisfies. The sad irony is that what the job seeker is willing to do to the employer—make a promise and then break it—he or she would be outraged to have done to him- or herself: have the job offer pulled. It is a very bad way to begin a career. It suggests the individual has not taken the time to do the necessary self-assessment and self-awareness exercises to think and judge critically. The new offer taken may, in fact, be no better or worse than the one refused. You should be aware that there have been incidents of legal action following job candidates' reneging on an offer. This adds a very sour note to what should be a harmonious beginning of a lifelong adventure.

CHAPTER EIGHT

THE GRADUATE SCHOOL CHOICE

T he reasons for furthering one's education in graduate school can be as varied and unique as the individuals electing this course of action. Many continue their studies at an advanced level because they simply find it difficult to end the educational process. They love what they are learning and want to learn more and broaden their academic exploration.

. . . .

Studying a particular subject, such as theories and patterns of intercultural communication, in great depth and thinking, researching, and writing critically on what others have discovered can provide excitement, challenge, and serious work. Some communications majors have loved this aspect of their academic work and want to continue that activity.

Others go on to graduate school for purely practical reasons; they have examined employment prospects in their field of study, and all indications are that a graduate degree is requisite. If you have earned a B.A. in communications as a stepping stone to a career in law or the foreign service, going on for further training becomes mandatory. As a B.A.-level speech pathologist, you realize you cannot become state certified without a master's degree. A review of jobs in different areas will suggest that at least a master's degree in the media, in editing, writing, or publishing can be a good source of what degree level the fields are hiring. Ask your college career office for some alumni names, and give them a telephone call. Prepare some questions on specific job prospects in their field at each degree level. A thorough examination of the marketplace and a conversation with employers and professors will give you a sense of the scope of employment for a bachelor's degree, master's degree, or doctorate.

College teaching will require and advanced degree. Advertising might demand specialization in an additional field (computers, graphic design, and so forth). Editing and publishing and other fields may well put a premium on the advanced degree because the market is over-supplied and the employer can afford to make this demand.

CONSIDER YOUR MOTIVES

The answer to the question of "Why graduate school?" is a personal one for each applicant. Nevertheless, it is important to consider your motives carefully. Graduate school involves additional time out of the employment market, a high level of critical evaluation, significant autonomy as you pursue your studies, and considerable financial expenditure. For some students in doctoral programs, there may be additional life choice issues, such as relationships, marriage, and parenthood, that may present real challenges while in a program of study. You would be well advised to consider the following questions as you think about your decision to continue your studies.

Are You Postponing Some Tough Decisions by Going to School?

Graduate school is not a place to go to avoid life's problems. There is intense competition for graduate school slots and for the fellowships, scholarships, and financial aid available. This competition means extensive interviewing, resume submission, and essay writing that rivals corporate recruitment. Likewise, the graduate school process is a mentored one in which faculty stay aware of and involved in the academic progress of their students and continually challenge the quality of their work. Many graduate students are called upon to participate in teaching and professional writing and research as well.

In other words, this is no place to hide from the spotlight. Graduate students work very hard and much is demanded of them individually. If you elect to go to graduate school to avoid the stresses and strains of the "real world," you will find no safe place in higher academics. Vivid accounts, both fictional and nonfictional, have depicted quite accurately the personal and professional demands of graduate school work.

The selection of graduate studies as a career option should be a positive choice—something you *want* to do. It shouldn't be selected as an escape from other, less attractive or more challenging options, nor should it be selected as the option of last resort (i.e., "I can't do anything else; I'd better just stay in school."). If you're in some doubt about the strength of your reasoning about continuing in school, discuss the issues with a career counselor. Together you can clarify your reasoning, and you'll get some sound feedback on what you're about to undertake.

On the other hand, staying on in graduate school because of a particularly poor employment market and a lack of jobs at entry-level positions has proved to be an effective "stalling" strategy. If you can afford it, pursuing a graduate degree immediately after your undergraduate education gives you a year or two to "wait out" a difficult economic climate, while at the same time acquiring a potentially valuable credential.

Have You Done Some "Hands-On" Reality Testing?
There are experiential options available to give some reality to your decision-making process about graduate school. Internships or work in the field can give you a good idea about employment demands, conditions, and atmosphere.

· ·

Perhaps, as a communications major, you're considering going on to law school. An internship or summer job in a law firm will put you in contact with practicing attorneys and may help to define for you exactly what attorneys do. Even with the experience of only one law firm, you have a stronger concept of the pace of the job, interaction with colleagues, subject matter, and opportunities for specialization. Talking to people and asking questions is invaluable as an exercise to help you better understand the objective of your graduate study.

For communications majors especially, the opportunity to do this kind of reality testing is invaluable. It demonstrates far more authoritatively than any other method what your real-world skills are, how they can be put to use, and what aspect of your academic preparation you rely on. It has been well documented that communications majors do well in occupations once they identify them. Internships and co-op experiences speed that process up and prevent the frustrating and expensive process of investigation many graduates begin only after graduation.

••

Do You Need an Advanced Degree to Work in Your Field?

Certainly there are fields such as law, psychiatry, medicine, and college teaching that demand advanced degrees. Is the field of employment you're considering one that also puts a premium on an advanced degree? You may be surprised. Read job ads on the Internet and in a number of major Sunday newspapers for positions you would enjoy. How many of those require an advanced degree?

Retailing, for example, has always put a premium on what people can do rather than how much education they have had. Successful people in retailing come from all academic preparations. A Ph.D. in your field may bring more prestige to a job, but it may not bring a more senior position or better pay. In fact, it may disqualify you for some jobs because an employer might believe you will be unhappy to be overqualified for a particular position. Or your motives in applying for the work may be misconstrued, and the employer might think you will only be working at this level until something better comes along. None of this may be true for you, but it comes about because you are working outside of the usual territory for that degree level.

When economic times are especially difficult, we tend to see stories featured about individuals with advanced degrees doing what is considered unsuitable work, such as the Ph.D. in French driving a cab or the Ph.D. in chemistry waiting tables. Actually, this is not particularly surprising when you consider that as your degree level advances, the job market narrows appreciably. At any one time, regardless of economic circumstances, there are only so many jobs for your particular level of expertise. If you cannot find employment for your advanced degree level, chances are you will be considered suspect for many other kinds of employment and may be forced into temporary work far removed from your original intention.

Before making an important decision such as graduate study, learn your options and carefully consider what you want to do with your advanced degree. Ask yourself whether it is reasonable to think you can achieve your goals. Will there be jobs when you graduate? Where will they be? What will they pay? How competitive will the market be at that time, based on current predictions?

If you're uncertain about the degree requirements for the fields you're interested in, you should check a publication such as the U.S. Department of Labor's *Occupational Outlook Handbook* (www.bls.gov). Each entry on the *OOH* includes a section on training and other qualifications that will indicate clearly what the minimum educational requirement is for employment, what degree is the standard, and what employment may be possible without the required credential.

For example, for physicists and astronomers a doctoral degree in physics or a closely related field is essential. Certainly this is the degree of choice in academic institutions. However, the *Occupational Outlook Handbook* also indicates what kinds of employment may be available to individuals holding a master's or even a bachelor's degree in physics.

Have You Compared Your Expectations of What Graduate School Will Do for You with What It Has Done for Alumni of the Program You're Considering?

Most colleges and universities perform some kind of postgraduate survey of their students to ascertain where they are employed, what additional education they have received, and what levels of salary they are enjoying. Ask to see this information either from the university you are considering applying to or from your own alma mater, especially if it has a similar graduate program. Such surveys often reveal surprises about occupational decisions, salaries, and work satisfaction. This information may affect your decision.

The value of self-assessment (the process of examining and making decisions about your own hierarchy of values and goals) is especially important in analyzing the desirability of possible career paths involving graduate education. Sometimes a job requiring advanced education seems to hold real promise but is disappointing in salary potential or number of opportunities available. Certainly it is better to research this information before embarking on a program of graduate studies. It may not change your mind about your decision, but by becoming better informed about your choice, you become better prepared for your future.

Have You Talked with People in Your Field to Explore What You Might Be Doing After Graduate School?

In pursuing your undergraduate degree, you will have come into contact with many individuals trained in the field you are considering. You might also have the opportunity to attend professional conferences, workshops, seminars, and job fairs where you can expand your network of contacts. Talk to them all! Find out about their individual career paths, discuss your own plans and hopes, get their feedback on the reality of your expectations, and heed their advice about your prospects. Each will have a unique tale to tell, and each will bring a different perspective on the current marketplace for the credentials you are seeking. Talking to enough people will make you an expert on what's out there.

Are You Excited by the Idea of Studying the Particular Field You Have in Mind?

This question may be the most important one of all. If you are going to spend several years in advanced study, perhaps engendering some debt or postponing some lifestyle decisions for an advanced degree, you simply ought to enjoy what you're doing. Examine your work in the discipline so far. Has it been fun? Have you found yourself exploring various paths of thought? Do you read in your area for fun? Do you enjoy talking about it, thinking about it, and sharing it with others? Advanced degrees often are the beginning of a lifetime's involvement with a particular subject. Choose carefully a field that will hold your interest and your enthusiasm.

If nothing else, do the following:

- Talk and question (remember to listen!)

- Reality test

- Soul-search by yourself or with a person you trust

FINDING THE RIGHT PROGRAM FOR YOU: SOME CONSIDERATIONS

There are several important factors in coming to a sound decision about the right graduate program for you. You'll want to begin by locating institutions that offer appropriate programs, examining each of these programs and their requirements, undertaking the application process by reviewing catalogs and obtaining application materials, visiting campuses if possible, arranging for letters of recommendation, writing your application statement, and, finally, following up on your applications.

Locate Institutions with Appropriate Programs

Once you decide on a particular advanced degree, it's important to develop a list of schools offering such a degree program. Perhaps the best source of graduate program information is Peterson's. The website (www.petersons .com) and the printed *Guides to Graduate Study* allow you to search for information by institution name, location, or academic area. The website also allows you to do a keyword search. Use the website and guides to build your list. In addition, you may want to consult the College Board's *Index of Majors and Graduate Degrees*, which will help you find graduate programs offering the degree you seek. It is indexed by academic major and then categorized by state.

Now, this may be a considerable list. You may want to narrow the choices down further by a number of criteria: tuition, availability of financial aid, public versus private institutions, United States versus international institutions, size of student body, size of faculty, application fee, and geographic location. This is only a partial list; you will have your own important considerations. Perhaps you are an avid scuba diver and you find it unrealistic to think you could pursue graduate study for a number of years without being able to ocean dive from time to time. Good! That's a decision and it's honest. Now, how far from the ocean is too far, and what schools meet your other needs? In any case, and according to your own criteria, begin to put together a reasonable list of graduate schools that you are willing to spend time investigating.

Examine the Degree Programs and Their Requirements

Once you've determined the criteria by which you want to develop a list of graduate schools, you can begin to examine the degree program requirements, faculty composition, and institutional research orientation. Again, using resources such as Peterson's website or guides can reveal an amazingly rich level of material by which to judge your possible selections.

In addition to degree programs and degree requirements, entries will include information about application fees, entrance test requirements, tuition, percentage of applicants accepted, numbers of applicants receiving financial aid, gender breakdown of students, numbers of full- and part-time faculty, and often gender breakdown of faculty as well. Numbers graduating in each program and research orientations of departments are also included in some entries. There is information on graduate housing; student services; and library, research, and computer facilities. A contact person, phone number, and address are also standard information in these listings.

It can be helpful to draw up a chart and enter relevant information about each school you are considering in order to have a ready reference on points of information that are important to you.

Undertake the Application Process

Program Information. Once you've decided on a selection of schools, obtain program information and applications. Nearly every school has a website that contains most of the detailed information you need to narrow your choices. In addition, applications can be printed from the site. If, however, you don't want to print out lots of information, you can request that a copy of the catalog and application materials be sent to you.

When you have your information in hand, give it all a careful reading and make notes of issues you might want to discuss via E-mail, on the telephone, or in a personal interview.

••

If you are interested in graduate work in intercultural communications, for example, in addition to graduate courses in anthropology, what other supplemental courses will you be required to take?

••

What is the ratio of faculty to the required number of courses for your degree? How often will you encounter the same faculty member as an instructor?

If the program offers a practicum or off-campus experience, who arranges this? Does the graduate school select a site and place you there, or is it your responsibility? What are the professional affiliations of the faculty? Does the program merit any outside professional endorsement or accreditation?

Critically evaluate the catalogs of each of the programs you are considering. List any questions you have and ask current or former teachers and colleagues for their impressions as well.

The Application. Preview each application thoroughly to determine what you need to provide in the way of letters of recommendation, transcripts from undergraduate schools or any previous graduate work, and personal essays. Make a notation for each application of what you will need to complete that document.

Additionally, you'll want to determine entrance testing requirements for each institution and immediately arrange to register for appropriate tests. Information can be obtained from associated websites, including www.ets.org (GRE, GMAT, TOEFL, PRAXIS, SLS, Higher Education Assessment), www.lsat.org (LSAT), and www.tpcweb.com/mat (MAT). Your college career office should also be able to provide you with advice and additional information.

Visit the Campus if Possible

If time and finances allow, a visit, interview, and tour can help make your decision easier. You can develop a sense of the student body, meet some of the faculty, and hear up-to-date information on resources and the curriculum. You will have a brief opportunity to "try out" the surroundings to see if they fit your needs. After all, it will be home for a while. If a visit is not possible but you have questions, don't hesitate to call and speak with the dean of the graduate school. Most are more than happy to talk to candidates and want them to have the answers they seek. Graduate school admission is a very personal and individual process.

Arrange for Letters of Recommendation

This is also the time to begin to assemble a group of individuals who will support your candidacy as a graduate student by writing letters of recommendation or completing recommendation forms. Some schools will ask you to provide letters of recommendation to be included with your application or sent directly to the school by the recommender. Other graduate programs will provide a recommendation form that must be completed by the recommender. These graduate school forms vary greatly in the amount of space provided for a written recommendation. So that you can use letters as you need to, ask your recommenders to address their letters "To Whom It May Concern," unless one of your recommenders has a particular connection to one of your graduate schools or knows an official at the school.

Choose recommenders who can speak authoritatively about the criteria important to selection officials at your graduate school. In other words, choose recommenders who can write about your grasp of the literature in your field of study, your ability to write and speak effectively, your class performance, and your demonstrated interest in the field outside of class. Other characteristics that graduate schools are interested in assessing include your emotional maturity, leadership ability, breadth of general knowledge, intellectual ability, motivation, perseverance, and ability to engage in independent inquiry.

When requesting recommendations, it's especially helpful to put the request in writing. Explain your graduate school intentions and express some of your thoughts about graduate school and your appreciation for their support. Don't be shy about "prompting" your recommenders with some suggestions of what you would appreciate being included in their comments. Most recommenders will find this direction helpful and will want to produce a statement of support that you can both stand behind. Consequently, if your interaction with one recommender was especially focused on research projects, he or she might be best able to speak of those skills and your critical thinking ability. Another recommender may have good comments to make about your public presentation skills.

Give your recommenders plenty of lead time in which to complete your recommendation, and set a date by which they should respond. If they fail to meet your deadline, be prepared to make a polite call or visit to inquire if they need more information or if there is anything you can do to move the process along.

Whether or not you are providing a graduate school form or asking for an original letter to be mailed, be sure to provide an envelope and postage if the recommender must mail the form or letter directly to the graduate school.

Each recommendation you request should provide a different piece of information about you for the selection committee. It might be pleasant for letters of recommendation to say that you are a fine, upstanding individual, but a selection committee for graduate school will require specific information. Each recommender has had a unique relationship with you, and his or her letter should reflect that. Think of each letter as helping to build a more complete portrait of you as a potential graduate student.

Write Your Application Statement

•••••••••••••••••••••••••••••••••••••

Many graduate applications require a personal statement. For a communications major, this should be an exciting and challenging assignment and one you should be able to complete successfully. Certainly, any required essay on a graduate application for communications will weigh heavily in the decision process of the graduate school admissions committee.

•••••••••••••••••••••••••••••••••••••

An excellent source to help in writing this essay is *How to Write a Winning Personal Statement for Graduate and Professional School,* by Richard J. Stelzer. It has been written from the perspective of what graduate school selection committees are looking for when they read these essays. It provides helpful tips to keep your essay targeted on the kinds of issues and criteria that are important to selection committees and that provide them with the kind of information they can best utilize in making their decision.

Follow Up on Your Applications

After you have finished each application and mailed it along with your transcript requests and letters of recommendation, be sure to follow up on the progress of your file. For example, call the graduate school administrative staff to see whether your transcripts have arrived. If the school required your recommenders to fill out a specific recommendation form that had to be mailed directly to the school, you will want to ensure that they have all arrived in good time for the processing of your application. It is your responsibility to make certain that all required information is received by the institution.

RESEARCHING FINANCIAL AID SOURCES, SCHOLARSHIPS, AND FELLOWSHIPS

Financial aid information is available from each graduate school. You may be eligible for federal, state, and/or institutional support. There are lengthy forms to complete, and some of these will vary by school, type of school (public versus private), and state. Be sure to note the deadline dates on each form.

There are many excellent resources available to help you explore all of your financial aid options. Visit your college career office or local public library to find out about the range of materials available. Two excellent resources are Peterson's website (www.petersons.com) and its book *Peterson's Grants for Graduate and Post Doctoral Study*. Another good reference is the Foundation Center's *Foundation Grants to Individuals*. These types of resources generally contain information that can be accessed by indexes including field of study, specific eligibility requirements, administering agency, and geographic focus.

EVALUATING ACCEPTANCES

If you apply to and are accepted at more than one school, it is time to return to your initial research and self-assessment to evaluate your options and select the program that will best help you achieve the goals you set for pursuing graduate study. You'll want to choose a program that will allow you to complete your studies in a timely and cost-effective way. This may be a good time to get additional feedback from professors and career professionals who are familiar with your interests and plans. Ultimately, the decision is yours, so be sure you get answers to all the questions you can think of.

SOME NOTES ABOUT REJECTION

Each graduate school is searching for applicants who appear to have the qualifications necessary to succeed in its program. Applications are evaluated on a combination of undergraduate grade point average, strength of letters of recommendation, standardized test scores, and personal statements written for the application.

A carelessly completed application is one reason many applicants are denied admission to a graduate program. To avoid this type of needless rejection, be sure to carefully and completely answer all appropriate questions on the application form, focus your personal statement given the instructions provided, and submit your materials well in advance of the deadline. Remember that your test scores and recommendations are considered a part of your application, so they must also be received by the deadline.

If you are rejected by a school that especially interests you, you may want to contact the dean of graduate studies to discuss the strengths and weaknesses of your application. Information provided by the dean will be useful in reapplying to the program later or applying to other, similar programs.

PART TWO

THE CAREER PATHS

CHAPTER NINE

INTRODUCTION TO THE COMMUNICATIONS CAREER PATHS

C ommunications is all about getting the word out—and there are as many ways to do that as there are words. Twenty years ago a bachelor's degree in English was sufficient to launch a successful career. While English majors still aggressively enter the marketplace, many employers view communications majors as better equipped to contribute to a fast-changing, information-based environment.

Communications opens more doors than any other major. With an understanding of how to penetrate public awareness and mold and respond to public opinion, communications can be public relations. With the knowledge of how to reach and influence consumers, communications can be advertising or publicity and promotion. Through the techniques of writing and editing, communications can be journalism. With problem-solving and group-management skills, communications can be corporate troubleshooting or training. And, for individuals working with communication disorders, communications can be speech-language pathology or audiology.

Communications majors can also use their undergraduate degree as a steppingstone to careers in medicine, education, law, government, or diplomacy. No other major offers as much flexibility.

CHOOSING THE RIGHT COMMUNICATIONS PROGRAM

There are almost as many different names and focuses for communication programs as there are job possibilities. Some common names are: communication studies, communication processes, communication science, speech communication, speech and mass communication, communication arts and speech, and communication disorders.

The colleges and universities that offer communications as a major house those departments in a variety of slots. In some institutions you will find the communications department encased within colleges of liberal arts. Others have separate communications schools. Still others combine communications within the school of journalism, or with advertising, public relations, or other related disciplines. In some universities, you will even find outreach programs, noncredit-bearing, adult education communications departments, whose aim is to teach new skills or upgrade the existing skills of people already out in the workforce.

The program or department name will not always be an accurate clue to its focus. A potential promotional campaign developer would waste precious time enrolling in a communication studies program that emphasized broadcasting or journalism.

As examples, two university communications departments are highlighted here to show how different institutions focus their curriculum.

The University of Florida, Gainesville

The University of Florida's communication studies (CS) program is housed within the Department of Communication Processes and Disorders in the College of Liberal Arts and Sciences. According to the description in the undergraduate handbook:

> The CS program provides students with both a theoretical and practical understanding of symbolic interaction and human communication processes. Communication includes both strategic and inadvertent meaning to those behaviors in transactional contexts. The communication studies program emphasizes theory, research, and practice in a diversity of communication systems, including: interpersonal relationships, small groups engaged in problem solving and decision making, and public communication. These communication systems are found in many contexts and that is reflected in the courses (e.g., the family, personal and social relationships, businesses and organizations, politics, national and intercultural encounters, urban relationships, and health care and promotion).

To simplify the above description, Dr. Anthony Clark, director of undergraduate studies at the University of Florida, Gainesville, talks about the program and its practical applications:

"Our program takes an open-ended approach; we're not a career-specific major. Our goal is to turn out an undergraduate student who is marketable, who will be picked up by Westinghouse or Xerox or Coca Cola, and then continue his or her training while on the job. We provide a good, solid grounding in contemporary communication. What we hope is that, when people interview for various careers, the person conducting the interview will sense that 'hey, this is a good bet for us. We can take this person and train him to do what we need,' as opposed to just picking them up and expecting them to hit the ground running.

"There are a lot of other majors, such as speech pathology for example, where the day you walk off the stage with your diploma, you're ready to do your job for the next fifty years. The problem with many other areas in communications is that there's no particular job title. It's almost like with the military—if it doesn't have a name it doesn't exist. If someone is a lawyer or a CPA we have a good idea what he or she does. If you call yourself a communicologist or communications specialist or corporate communicator, it's hard to pinpoint exactly what it is you do. It's hard to identify. But in corporations, they know who they're talking about when they get this kind of person.

"Because it's a relatively new enterprise and because it goes across a wide range of career opportunities, we still need some labelers and identifiers. But we're hoping that by grounding people very thoroughly in the rudiments and then putting some polish on that they will be seen as marketable.

"Although there are others, we have two major tracks: public communications and interpersonal communications.

"The former often leads to work with service organizations. Our graduates develop promotional campaigns for the National Institute of Health or the Center for Disease Control in Atlanta. They work with the American Cancer Society, the American Red Cross, or Easter Seals.

"The majority of our students enter the interpersonal communications track. Most graduates go into business and are hired by large companies, serving the hotel industry, entertainment, and travel, for example.

"We find that communications studies majors are more and more marketable in these areas. Not too long ago, the national headquarters of the Revlon Corporation asked for a list of our graduating seniors. They want people who are skilled in the kinds of areas we teach. The same thing is true with bank chains. They are not interested so much anymore in finance or accounting majors because they have all that machinery and high tech equipment to do much of that work. What they want now are individuals who are trained more in interpersonal skills and who are trained in group problem solving, conflict management, and mediation, which is what we cover in our program."

What follows is a sampling of some of the University of Florida's communication studies courses:

Introduction to communication studies

Interpersonal communication in health care and promotion

Public speaking

Nonverbal communication

Argumentation

Small group communication

Issues in public deliberation

Another track within the University of Florida's program is a focus on communication or communicative disorders. Students in this program, both undergraduate and graduate, learn about disorders and pathology affecting individuals. Graduates go into careers as speech pathologists or audiologists.

The University of Wisconsin, Madison

The University of Wisconsin, Madison, has schools and departments where students can pursue communications studies, explore traditional journalism and mass communications, as well as agricultural journalism and communications arts.

The communications program is housed within the university outreach division. It is a noncredit-bearing, continuing education course of study aimed at adults who arc already working in various fields or are considering a career change. Students in credit-bearing departments also take advantage of the outreach program's curriculum.

Marshall J. Cook, former chairman and current full professor in the department and author, explains their focus:

"In the division of outreach we cover health and human issues, humanities, and speech and organizational communications. We're eclectic, and we put the stress on teaching. We offer workshops in journalism and mass communications—freelance writing, publishing, and some print design and production. We also provide training on the Internet and in public speaking.

"Primarily, although not entirely, we are dealing with professionals who already have jobs. Others are looking into changing careers. They come to broaden their skills or learn new ones. For example, an employee in a company has just been told he is now responsible for putting out the in-house newsletter. It might be a small company without any employees versed in these areas. He comes to us to learn how to do it.

"In my area we work with staff writers, editors, business and industry people who work on house publications, public relations people, freelancers, fiction writers, and people who are trying to find a publisher or are considering self-publishing.

"In our speech and organizational communications section we work with government entities, university and business people, marketing professionals, and a lot of nonprofit service organizations. They have a great need but not a whole lot of money. It's more cost-effective to train one of their own than to hire an additional professional.

"Our program stresses personal and professional development and has an impact on the economy of the state. We help publications that want to improve and turn a profit, and assist government agencies in working more effectively.

"We do a lot of the nuts-and-bolts stuff that many campuses don't cover. You can go through a four-year program and never learn how to write a query letter, or even learn what one is, or how to market yourself and your work, or some important hands-on computer skills.

"Communications is an evolving field and our curriculum reflects the interests of our faculty and of the community. Basically our aim is to offer a good quality continuing education program."

What follows is a sampling of some of the University of Wisconsin's outreach communication programs' workshops:

Interpersonal and workplace communication

Marketing and media relations

Nonprofit development

Marketing your writing

Low-budget filmmaking

Report writing

Communicative disorders

Because of the wide diversity of programs, communications majors cannot afford to wait to make a career path decision until *after* they enroll at a university. The desired field of study must at least be narrowed down to a fairly specific focus before one sends out applications for admission.

Consulting course catalogs and talking with instructors and other students will show how content materials are organized at the various institutions offering communications majors. Knowing what path you want to follow, then choosing the best university to match your needs, will help ensure you get started on the right track.

The remainder of this book is devoted to exploring a selection of career paths and the actual jobs within those paths.

THE CAREER PATHS

What college student doesn't hope to find a great job upon graduation? With four years of study and careful planning throughout your college program, there is no reason why, as a communications major, you shouldn't walk into the plum job of your choosing.

There are a lot of choices, however, and the aim of this book is to help you narrow them down and find the career path that best suits your education, interests, and skills.

For the purposes of this book, four main paths are explored, but they are in no way exhaustive. As you have already gleaned from reading the introduction to this book, the list of main tracks numbers close to two dozen. Within those tracks are thousands of different job titles. Many are explored throughout the following four chapters, as primary paths or secondary and related paths.

The four career paths described in this book are:

1. Corporate communications

2. Consumer communications

3. Media

4. Communication disorders

As mentioned previously, this list is by no means comprehensive. Many university programs allow for a great deal of latitude in designing majors and courses of study. It is now common practice to pursue interdisciplinary degrees. With a little bit of guidance and creativity, you should be able to make a case for your communications degree in any area you wish to enter.

CHAPTER TEN

PATH 1: CORPORATE COMMUNICATIONS

The corporate world is wide-open territory for communications majors. If you take the simplest definition of communications as "getting the word out," the corporate community has one of the largest uses of this activity. Some sectors need to get the message out in-house through newsletters, memos, position papers, letters from the president, corporate training, seminars, and workshops; other sectors need to get the message out to the public or to consumers, through conventions, advertisements, publicity campaigns, community relations, or media contacts.

A survey of state universities throughout the United States reveals that the top two majors students are currently pursuing are 1) business and 2) communications. Aspects of the two majors are closely related. Although some business majors focus their training in areas of banking and finance, many others choose to pursue careers identical to those prepared for by communications majors. Equally, a significant number of communications majors choose a university department and career track that will lead them into jobs in business settings.

The process of getting the word out can use the skills of just one person or employ teams of ten, fifty, or a hundred professionals. Their job titles and the roles they play are as varied as the messages they are striving to convey.

DEFINITION OF THE CAREER PATH

The profession of communications is difficult to define, and, these days, it is easier to say what it isn't. Norman Leaper, past president of the International Association of Business Communicators (IABC), in a recent speech remarked: "The role of communication has changed . . . [It was] a term that . . . conjured up visions of company-produced newsletters by folks whose idea of creativity was a Christmas message printed in the shape of a tree in green ink. Or maybe a series of press releases extolling the virtues of a new fertilizer. . . . No longer is it considered an insecure entry in the budget . . . [or a] luxury or a frill delegated to secretaries who like to write. . . .

"It has become one of the most important elements in any organization . . . an essential link between managers and workers . . . a liaison between employees and the broader community. . . .

"Management is realizing that good, timely, candid communication is a sound investment both within and outside the organization."

The focus of this chapter is on the varied roles communications majors can play in the corporate world.

Public Relations

The field of public relations is relatively young, formally founded less than a hundred years ago. Early definitions emphasized public relations as press agentry and publicity. As the profession evolved, those aspects became less the work of the PR professional, falling more into the realm of publicists and advertising and marketing professionals. (This area is covered in Chapter 11.)

Today, public relations is a huge umbrella under which a variety of job titles and professional responsibilities exist. Modern public relations embraces the consultant, corporate communicator, investor relations specialist, public information officer, community liaison, government mediator, troubleshooter, spokesperson, and media coordinator.

The number of professionals doing public relations work is estimated to be about 130,000. Public relations professionals work in every sector, from the corporate world to the sporting world, from government departments to health and medical facilities. And though the settings might vary, their main responsibility usually doesn't. The backbone of every PR professional's job description is his or her role as communicator.

Effective communications are recognized as vital to the success of every organization or cause. Every organization has "publics" to which it must answer. Let's take for an example a large movie theater concern that we'll call National Cinema Corporation. The "publics" that National Cinema Corporation must stay sensitive to include nutritionists and other health professionals who insist that consumers be informed about the fat content of movie theater popcorn; environmentalists who insist that the containers used for the popcorn and cold drinks be biodegradable, or that the tickets be printed on recycled paper; city and town planners who are concerned about parking facilities and traffic patterns near the movie theater as well as signage and lighting; civic groups that are lobbying for improved movie rating systems; zoning officials and school officials—the list can go on and on.

Excluded from this list are customers or consumers, a public that is attended to by professionals involved in advertising, marketing, opinion research, publicity, and promotion and is categorized separately.

The public relations professional is concerned with how the company is perceived by the various target audiences. He or she can also help shape a company and the way it performs. The PR practitioner, by research and evaluation, finds out the expectations and concerns of the various groups and reports back to the organization on his or her findings. A good public relations program needs the support of the organization and the public it is involved with.

The Public Relations Society of America offers accreditation to PR professionals who have been in the field, either in practice or teaching in an accredited college or university for a period of time not less than five years. After candidates pass a written and oral examination to demonstrate their competence and knowledge, they are given the right to use the designation PRSA Accredited or APR. This adds to their professional credibility and personal confidence.

Many of the following job titles fall under the umbrella of professional public relations.

Corporate Communicators

Corporate communicators come with a variety of job titles and perform a mixed bag of functions. As troubleshooters, they handle communication disorders within organizations, acting as problem solvers, group facilitators, negotiators, and mediators. In this capacity, they can also be concerned with keeping professional morale high and keeping workers energized and creative. Whether as an in-house employee or as an independent consultant, a corporate communicator specializing in disorders will conduct a needs-analysis and then design and implement a program to tackle the specific problem. For example, corporate communicators at Exxon conduct seminars for managers to heighten awareness of the concerns of minority and female employees. Various methods and techniques are used such as role-playing, values clarification, simulations, and other hands-on exercises. AT&T instituted an open line for employees to voice their concerns and complaints. Southwestern Bell Telephone arranged for its managers to appear on radio talk shows to respond to complaints and questions from listeners.

Corporate communicators, functioning much as PR specialists, would also act as external troubleshooters, handling problems that develop between an organization and the community within which it is located. Experience has shown that readily sharing information with the community and the media, as well as with employees, can turn around relationships initially based on strife and conflict into working, productive alliances. Atlantic Richfield publishes a weekly newspaper read by approximately 76,000 employees around the world. Among other newsworthy events, the paper reports on deaths resulting from company accidents, details of unfavorable lawsuits, competition in the field, and analyses of the causes for depressed stock prices.

AT&T Technologies is another example of a company that recognizes the importance of candor. It developed a guide for its spokespersons, advising them to be forthright with the press and pointing out that the company's interests are served best by volunteering bad news instead of trying to cover it up.

A major accident at a chemical plant in Martinez, California, in 1992 is a good illustration of how this works. Two maintenance workers accidentally opened a valve on a tank storing spent sulfuric acid. One of the workers was killed and the fires resulting from the spill shut down a major freeway. Because the community had already been in a four-year battle with the company, opposing a permit to incinerate hazardous waste, the accident spurred panic and anger. Company spokespersons handled the crisis with sincere apologies and a constant, ongoing availability of information to the press and the community. After two years, the open communication and a change of attitude and management improved relations between the company and the community to such a point that both sides feel there is now an atmosphere of trust and confidence.

In addition to problem-solving roles, corporate communicators can also be hired to work in the area of multimedia communications, both in-house and external. IABC past president Norman Leaper notes that, "Progressive organizations have replaced self-serving news releases and publications featuring pompous pep talks on productivity with communication programs that include sophisticated films, videotapes, and other audio-visual efforts; bulletin board presentations; telephone news systems and hotlines; and literally scores of other forms of communication that reach millions of people within and outside the organization."

Corporate communicators arrange news conferences, conduct surveys, produce radio or TV news shows, arrange monthly "gripe" sessions between management and staff, design brochures describing the company's strengths and aims, write speeches for the CEO to deliver to stockholders, arrange seminars and workshops, edit glossy magazines, or initiate programs to ensure workplace safety or increase environmental awareness.

Corporate communicators interested in editing and publishing have an estimated 30,000 internal and external organizational publications to approach throughout the United States and Canada. Only 20 percent of consumer magazines hire new grads right out of college, and when they do, they usually position the new staff in low-responsibility slots. Communications majors entering the world of business get a shot at the whole show, from planning features to choosing illustrations.

What follows is an actual job advertisement for an experienced corporate communicator:

SENIOR EMPLOYEE: COMMUNICATIONS SPECIALIST

_____, named one of America's ten best employers, is seeking a rounded corporate communicator for its _____ office. The qualified applicant will be able to plan communication strategies, lead a writing team, edit/write for nationally recognized publications, and serve internal clients. Required is a degree in communications, journalism, or related field and five to ten years corporate/agency/newspaper experience to include heavy business writing. Must possess excellent skills in production and project management, communication planning, editing, writing, and interpersonal and client relations. Experience in managing print budgets and desktop publishing would be preferred.

_____offers excellent benefits, competitive salary, and a retirement plan. Salary history and resume should be mailed to . . .

Taking an entry-level position within a corporation is almost a guarantee of a start up the corporate ladder. Successful corporate communicators show initiative, creativity, and a strong sense of compassion and integrity. The larger the corporation, the more varied the duties, and the more chances of adding to your professional and personal skill bank.

Corporate communications is an exciting and challenging field of opportunities, opportunities that are particularly available to communications majors.

Intercultural Communications

With more and more American companies becoming global with multinational concerns, intercultural and cross-cultural communications have become important issues. Major corporations, such as Coca-Cola, have toeholds in almost every conceivable market in the world, from major markets in the Far East to isolated pockets in Africa or small island nations. In addition, international businesses based overseas deal with countries other than just the United States. Corporate Japan, for example, courts a lucrative market in

Korea, and the European Economic Community regularly conducts business across the geographical and cultural borders of Europe.

American communications majors play an important role in intercultural and cross-cultural communications. When a Pizza Hut opens its doors in a Persian Gulf country, it's an American intercultural communicator who goes there to ensure good relations between Arab franchise owners and Indian or Filipino workers.

The goal is to get the job done—without offending anyone. Intercultural communications experts work both at home and abroad. They deal with corporate managers or entry-level workers, teaching effective communication skills between cultures.

Corporate Training

Just as with corporate communicators, corporate trainers can put their skills to use in a variety of capacities. For example, before intercultural communicators can even begin to accomplish their employers' goals, they might have to spend months living in a culture, feeling their way through to becoming familiar with it. This is not the most effective and productive method. Instead, savvy companies hire the services of a corporate trainer who is already versed in the particular culture and environment. An expert corporate trainer will save a company time and uncountable dollars. A good trainer can teach a potential intercultural communicator most of what he or she needs to know in a matter of weeks, not months, and for far less money than an extended stay overseas would cost.

Corporate trainers also work strictly stateside, teaching communications skills between staff and management, conducting seminars and workshops, running motivational sessions, and teaching new skills and upgrading existing ones.

A corporate trainer could work with employees and a new computer system or provide orientation to new employees. The role of the corporate trainer can be as varied as the company's enterprises.

Investor Relations

Investor relations is a specialty within corporate communications for businesses that are owned by the public through the sale of stock. The investor relations professional makes sure that there is an open flow of information from the corporation to shareholders, prospective investors, financial analysts who make stock recommendations, lending institutions that issue lines of credit, and business and financial writers associated with the news media.

Investor relations practitioners might also be involved with the writing and distribution of quarterly and annual reports, and ensuring that the company adheres to regulations imposed on it by the Securities and Exchange Commission.

In addition to a strong communications background, candidates in this area must also have solid financial and investment expertise.

Government Relations

A government relations specialist puts PR techniques to good use when dealing with potential legislation that would negatively affect an organization. He or she can help to create public awareness or rally public opinion or sympathy to the cause.

Alumni Relations and Development

One of a university's biggest assets is its alumni. Both state- and privately funded institutions rely in part on donations from former students to meet budgetary needs. Most universities have departments staffed with professional communicators whose duties include locating and maintaining contact with alumni, coordinating regional alumni chapters, and helping to organize alumni events.

Communications take the form of personal letters, newsletters, magazines, and, sometimes, telephone calls, all appealing to the alumni's sense of school spirit and loyalty to the alma mater.

Fund-Raising and Event Coordination

For charitable organizations and other nonprofits, as well as political entities, fund-raising is a major activity. Here, communicators develop promotional campaigns and membership drives, stage events—charitable balls, dinners, speakers, Sunday softball league tournaments—and maintain media contact.

POSSIBLE JOB TITLES

The following list has been drawn up to give you an idea of the scope of jobs available in the corporate world that would be of interest to communications majors. There is much overlap, however, across occupations and job settings. For example, job titles within the field of public relations will also be found in health communications, and job titles that exist in a corporate setting also find a home within advertising agencies or marketing firms.

For ease in locating particular job titles, the list has been arranged alphabetically. However, this list is by no means exhaustive. During your job search, you can use this list as a reference, adding to it as you come across notices for jobs that mention related skills.

Alumni relations coordinator	Group/regional manager
Business development manager	Industrial PR executive
Civic affairs representative	Intercultural communications
Communications consultant	specialist
Communications specialist	Intercultural communicator
Community affairs coordinator	Interpersonal communicator
Community relations specialist	Investor relations director
Consumer affairs specialist	Management supervisor
Copyeditor	Patient advocate
Copywriter	Press secretary
Corporate communications	Promotional campaign developer
director	Public information officer
Corporate communicator	Public relations assistant
Director of development	Public relations manager
Editor	Public relations writer
Educational affairs director	Research assistant
Employee publications specialist	Researcher
Event coordinator	Spokesperson
Fund-raiser	Staff writer
Government relations	Volunteer coordinator

POSSIBLE EMPLOYERS

The International Association of Business Communicators surveyed 12,000 of its more than 13,700 members to determine the range of industries and types of businesses or organizations in which member communications professionals were employed. The majority, 40.51 percent, reported working for corporations. Other settings included the following:

Nonprofit associations: 12.72%

Consulting firms, communications: 8.06%

Self-employed/freelance: 5.62%

Utility companies: 4.60%

Educational institutions: 4.56%

Government/military: 4.34%

Consulting firms, management: 3.46%

Writing/editing firms: 1.15%

State-owned corporations: .99%

Labor unions: .14%

Other: 13.85%

The specific industries employing communications professionals included:

Advertising: 1.72%	Manufacturing: 5.54%
Aerospace: 1.31%	Medical/health: 8.44%
Agriculture: .67%	Metals/mining: .61%
Audiovisual: .70%	Petroleum: 1.60%
Automotive: .71%	Pharmaceutical: 1.27%
Chemical: 1.25%	Photography: .37%
Computers: 2.89%	Professional services: 3.27%
Construction: .29%	Public relations: 8.06%
Design: 1.34%	Publishing: 1.99%
Education: 5.02%	Real estate: .67%
Engineering: 1.35%	Retail sales: 1.23%
Finance/banking: 6.14%	Transportation: 1.86%
Food/beverage: 1.82%	Utilities (communications): 4.58%
Graphic arts/printing: 1.39%	Other: 24.07%
Hotel/lodging: .44%	
Insurance: 5.63%	

Though the distribution appears to be fairly evenly spread among these specific industries, the medical/health and public relations fields were out in front with an 8.44 and 8.06 percent.

Several of these settings are examined here and in later chapters in this book.

Corporations

Many large corporations place communication specialists within their personnel departments or human resources programs. Some corporations also have specific communications departments. In addition, communications specialists are commonly found within various other departments, such as advertising, publications, public relations, research and development, and sales.

Private Consulting Firms

More and more, private consulting firms are fulfilling a need for those corporations that, whether because of size or budget, do not choose to hire a permanent staff of corporate communicators, trainers, or PR professionals.

Private consulting firms work with clients on a fee-for-service basis or on a retainer. As needs or problems arise, a corporation can bring in a consulting firm that will conduct a needs analysis and submit a written proposal covering how they plan to proceed and how much it will cost.

Consultants employed by a firm can work on a straight salary basis or salary plus commission.

Private Public Relations Firms

Public relations firms function much the same way as private consulting firms do. They take on a variety of different clients, from large corporations to church groups or government bodies, assess their needs, propose a plan of action, and often implement that plan.

Most PR firms are located in major cities and have a staff size ranging from fewer than a dozen workers to more than one thousand. Some offices are generalists, while others specialize in specific areas such as government relations, employee communications, or educational and social programs.

Self-Employed/Freelancers

Self-employed or freelance communications consultants work similarly to their counterparts employed by private firms. The advantage is that the money to be made goes directly to the consultant and not into the firm's coffer; the disadvantage is that the independent consultant has to cover all of his or her own expenses and build up a client base from scratch.

Foreign Service

The foreign service is a natural choice for communications majors interested in business and intercultural communications. The foreign service divides the different specialty areas into the following categories:

Administration. Administrative personnel at overseas posts are responsible for hiring foreign national workers, providing office and residential space, ensuring reliable communications with the District of Columbia, supervising computer systems, and providing security for the post's personnel and property.

Consular Services. Consular workers must be excellent communicators and often combine the skills of lawyers, judges, investigators, and social workers.

Their duties range from issuing passports and visas to finding a lost child or helping a traveler in trouble.

Economic Officers. Economic officers maintain contact with key business and financial leaders in the host country, reporting to Washington on the local economic conditions and their impact on American trade and investment policies. They are concerned with issues such as commercial aviation safety, fishing rights, and international banking.

Political Affairs. Those working in political affairs analyze and report on the political views of the host country. They make contact with labor unions, humanitarian organizations, educators, and cultural leaders.

Information and Cultural Affairs. As part of the foreign service, the United States Information Agency (USIA) promotes U.S. cultural, informational, and public diplomacy programs. An information officer might develop a library open to the public, meet with the press, and oversee English language training programs in the host country.

Commercial and Business Services. In this division, a foreign service officer identifies overseas business connections for American exporters and investors, conducts market research for the success of U.S. products, and organizes trade shows and other promotional events.

Although many foreign service officers are skilled in political science and history, these days candidates are expected to have knowledge in specialized fields such as communications, the environment, computer science, and trade.

Government Agencies

Some readers may not initially associate working for government agencies with corporate communications. In actuality, the services the government needs are similar, if not identical, to those used in the business world. Internal employee relations and external public relations are concerns as important in the public sector as they are in the private sector. Although the job titles might vary—public information officer rather than PR specialist—the services they perform are the same.

In addition to the foreign service, there are scores of government agencies and departments on the local, state, and federal level that use the services of professional communicators.

Military

The military uses both civilian and noncivilian personnel in a variety of communications activities, from promotion and recruitment to public information and intelligence.

Public information officers (PIOs) deal with the community, media, and internal communications, usually in the form of base newsletters or other military publications. Intelligence agencies, both at home and abroad, employ communications specialists expert in gathering data and channeling them to the appropriate offices.

A stint in military communications is a career in itself or an excellent stepping stone to the corporate world.

Utilities

Utility companies no longer sit quietly in the background going about their business of providing power. Environmentalists (and the PR professionals who work for them) have raised public awareness to the dangers of potential and existing environmental hazards. PR professionals employed by utilities keep communication open, instituting programs to work with the community, and documenting and explaining their impact on the environment.

Communications majors in this field need to be skilled negotiators, as comfortable with a computer as a microphone.

Labor Unions

Labor unions recognize the importance of building support for their programs and positions. Major unions and their affiliates operate news and speaker bureaus; publish a variety of newsletters, reports, and brochures; and offer educational programs to civic groups and schools.

A communications major at home in this setting can find a satisfying lifelong career.

Nonprofit Associations

The term *nonprofit* is a tax status exempting some organizations from partial or complete tax payments; it was never intended to mean that a profit couldn't be made. Having said that, it is true that the nonprofit sector often has less money (and more need for it) than the private, profit-making sector. While salaries in these settings might be lower, the work experience can be equally, if not more, rewarding than in the corporate world.

Nonprofit associations number in the hundreds of thousands nationwide. Under this umbrella fall charitable organizations, private foundations, professional associations, and some educational institutions.

Charitable groups such as Easter Seals, the American Red Cross, the American Cancer Society, Big Brothers/Big Sisters, the United Way, YMCA and YWCA, Boy Scouts of America, the American Heart Association, and a score of others need employees with communications backgrounds.

And for every profession, there is at least one professional association, a membership-supported organization joining together groups of people with common interests and career goals. While most new graduates look upon professional associations as a place to get career support and perhaps help in finding a job, communications majors realize that this setting can be the ultimate career goal in itself.

Specialist communicators working for charitable organizations and professional associations perform much the same functions as their counterparts in the corporate world. Promotional campaigns need to be developed, media to be contacted, and employee and community relations need to be maintained. Added to this are the activities of fund-raising and membership drives.

Growth in this sector seems to be on the rise and more and more rewarding opportunities are becoming available.

Educational Institutions

Universities, colleges, and other educational institutions have a great need for employees with communications backgrounds. Here are just a few departments in which a communications major would be qualified to work:

- **Admissions:** This department communicates the highlights of the institution to attract new students.

- **Alumni Relations:** This office maintains contact with alumni for the purpose of fund-raising and community relations.

- **Career Placement/Service Centers:** Contact with potential employees is established here, and these professionals provide career counseling and guidance to students.

- **Community Affairs/Relations:** This department ensures open communication and cooperation between the institution and neighboring community, and develops outreach programs providing adult- and continuing-education programs.

- **Cooperative Education:** This office maintains contact with the business community and other fields for student job placement.

- **Development:** The ongoing process of fund-raising continues here, targeting other groups in addition to alumni.

- **International Student Affairs:** This office provides orientation, counseling, and help with immigration procedures to foreign students.

- **Publications:** These individuals work with campus newspapers, magazines, college catalogs, yearbooks, and other print needs of the institution.

In addition to being an employment setting for communications specialists, educational institutions offer the communications major—usually one with a Ph.D.—the added employment opportunity of teaching future communications majors.

Communications departments are flourishing; currently communications ranks second only to business as the most popular major. This means that there is a growing need for instructors and professors to teach the communication skills that are needed in the nonacademic world.

Hospitals and Medical Centers

The health care industry—and it is an industry—has a growing need for communications specialists to fill many of the same roles they would in the corporate world. With changes in national health care policies, the need for specialists in public relations, community affairs, marketing, and other related areas is on the increase.

Possible settings include:

Government-funded agencies (such as the Centers for Disease Control)

Pharmaceutical companies

Professional schools of medicine

Health advertising agencies

Rehabilitation clinics

Hospitals (both private and community based)

Residential treatment facilities

Volunteer health organizations

Outpatient medical centers

Job titles and responsibilities are similar to those in the corporate world. The main skill being sought is the ability to communicate effectively.

Here is an actual job advertisement for a position utilizing communications skills in a health care setting:

CRITICAL INQUIRY COORDINATOR

_____currently has an opportunity available for a critical inquiry coordinator with the critical inquiry department. This department is responsible for research, resolution, and response to formal grievances and appeals filed by clients and providers.

This position requires a conscientious individual with excellent communication and organizational skills. Outstanding skill in letter composition is a must. Candidate must possess a minimum of two years of college and related work experience or a bachelor's degree in communications, English, journalism, or health care administration. Send resume to . . .

As you start your own job search, you will see that the employment possibilities health care settings offer for communications majors are broad and stimulating.

RELATED OCCUPATIONS

The skills that communications majors possess are valued in a number of related professions. The following is a small sampling of occupations that draw on similar skills to a greater or lesser degree.

Biocommunications	In-house legal counsel
Development specialist	Lobbyist
Financial manager	Medical writer
Health science communications	Technical writer
Industrial psychologist	Volunteer coordinator

WORKING CONDITIONS

Corporations, public relations firms, and other possible employment settings are usually busy, hectic places. There are deadlines to be met, phones ringing, and visitors arriving, resulting in work schedules that are frequently interrupted. PR people and all the other corporate communicators put in long and sometimes irregular hours. Once a project is under way or a crisis needs to be resolved, the work seldom stops until the job is done.

Employees of nonprofit corporations, associations, and charitable organizations report to a calmer work atmosphere, but the pressure is on there as well. These organizations have the same need for effective communicators but a lot less money to accomplish their goals.

Workloads in the different settings will be varied, too. You could be hired to conduct a week's workshop on effective speaking and listening skills designed particularly for the phone company, and when you're finished, there's the company report to work on, letters to write, phone calls to return, meetings to attend, research to be done. The pace can be exhilarating and challenging to some, stress-producing to others.

TRAINING AND QUALIFICATIONS

For any of the fields covered in this chapter, a bachelor's degree in communications provides a good entry. However, while some positions, such as assistant/junior copywriters, don't require a four-year degree, as competition for jobs increases B.A.- or even master's-degree holders will have an edge. But a degree is not the only criterion an employer sets. The following skills have been identified in an IABC survey as those most commonly used by its membership:

Audience research	Magazine layout
Audiovisual production	Management skills
Budgeting/cost control	Media contact
Communication planning	Newsletter editing
Communication theory	Newswriting
Event planning	Personnel supervision
Feature writing	Photography
Feedback system design	Print production
Film production	Proposal writing
Government relations	Scriptwriting
Graphic design	Speakers bureaus
Identity programs	Speech writing
Investor relations	Time management

In addition, these other skills and personal qualities become important depending upon the area of business communications you choose to pursue. The more of these you are able to acquire or nurture, the better your chances of securing the type of job you are seeking.

Bilingual or multilingual abilities	Initiative
Compassion	Intelligence
Creativity	Integrity
Cross-cultural sensitivity	Interpersonal skills
Detail-orientation	Organizational skills
Drive	Research skills
Empathy	Verbal skills
Judgment	Writing skills

Some qualities people are born with; others can be acquired. Future communications specialists can start while in college. In addition to the courses required for the major, a host of other classes will enrich your skill bank and enhance your resume. These days, with more and more businesses and organizations entering the international marketplace, being fluent in one or more foreign languages can only work in your favor. Enroll in economics, finance, management, sociology, psychology, and public speaking.

Get as much practical hands-on experience as you can while in college. Work for the student newspaper or on the yearbook staff. Help organize student activities, volunteer for the speakers bureau, or become a peer counselor.

Participate in work-study or cooperative-education programs, and take advantage of any internships or practicums you are able to line up, even if it means extending your graduation date a semester. Most university programs cooperate with local, national, and sometimes international businesses to place students in hands-on internships. If your university does not have access to these kinds of placements, you can often arrange them on your own. A phone call or a letter to the right company could be all it takes to open the door to a rewarding experience.

Many successful communications specialists also have a record of volunteer service with civic groups and charities. For those seeking intercultural experiences, find summer employment overseas or after graduation do a stint in the Peace Corps. Teaching English as a foreign language overseas is a rewarding way to acquire cross-cultural experience. While on campus, interact with the international student office or volunteer in the English-as-a-second-language program. Intercultural sensitivity and experience can often be best gained outside the classroom.

While the job market is competitive, it is open to newcomers, especially to newcomers who have shown initiative in preparing themselves as much as possible.

CAREER OUTLOOK

Businesses and other organizations spend more than one billion dollars annually to communicate with employees or members, with even more money going to fund communication with external audiences such as customers, community residents, alumni, opinion leaders, and the public at large.

According to predictions made in the *Occupational Outlook Handbook*, published by the U.S. Department of Labor, Bureau of Labor Statistics, employment of corporate communications managers is expected to increase faster than the average for all occupations through the year 2008. Employment for public relations specialists other than managers is expected to increase faster than the average for all jobs through the year 2008.

Employment in public relations firms is expected to grow more than in any other setting, as corporations, trying to keep costs down, hire contractors to provide PR services rather than support a full-time communications staff.

Keen competition for these jobs, however, will likely continue among recent college graduates with degrees in communications and related fields because the number of applicants is expected to exceed the number of job openings. Although the job market has narrowed somewhat, many attractive opportunities are available to recent grads and demand for their skills remains strong.

EARNINGS

According to a recent College Placement Council Survey, entry-level salaries in public relations average about $21,000. Another comprehensive study, jointly conducted in 2000 by the International Association of Business Communicators and the Public Relations Society of America, shows that the average annual base salary for communicators is $69,000, with an average bonus of $10,000. Of course, salaries vary depending upon the region of the country and the size and budget of the hiring institution.

If the starting salaries seem disappointingly low, the good news is that as employees travel up the corporate ladder, salaries rise with them. Consultants' salaries are considerably higher than those with a corporate position, $110,000 versus $63,000. Consultants' cash bonuses are higher, too, averaging $20,000 versus $9,000 for those working in the corporate sector.

The following charts will give you an idea of your earning potential after a few years in a variety of settings.

MEDIAN AND AVERAGE SALARIES BY JOB TITLE

	Median	Average
President/exec. dir./CEO	$75,000	$135,000
Manager/asst. manager	56,000	56,000
Director	65,000	79,000
Specialist	39,000	41,000
Coordinator	35,000	37,500
Consultant	52,000	153,000
Vice president	95,000	149,000
Writer	45,000	50,000
Editor	51,000	48,000
Managing director	60,000	65,500
Independent/self-empl.	56,000	57,000
Group manager	60,000	60,000
Supervisor	51,000	45,000
Account exec.	36,500	36,000
Sr. account exec.	50,000	48,000
Senior/executive VP	100,000	125,864
Partner/principal/assoc.	150,000	97,000
Educator/professor	44,000	52,000

SALARY BY INDUSTRY

	Median	Average
Finance/banking	$57,000	$82,000
Medical/health care	46,000	79,500
Association/nonprofit	42,000	50,000
Insurance	50,000	60,500
Manufacturing	57,000	65,000
Education	43,000	53,000
Telecommunication	55,500	66,500
Consulting firm	61,000	79,650
Government	47,000	52,000
Utility (water/gas/energy)	61,000	74,000
Public relations	62,500	123,500
Computers	70,000	70,500
Prof. services	60,000	80,000
Transportation	47,500	52,500
Engineering	57,000	53,500

Public relations	62,500	123,500
Computers	70,000	70,500
Prof. services	60,000	80,000
Transportation	47,500	52,500
Engineering	57,000	53,500
Food/beverage	57,500	68,500
Advertising	52,500	50,500
Cultural/travel/tourism	39,000	48,000
Retail sales	69,000	67,500

SALARY BY YEARS IN THE COMMUNICATIONS FIELD

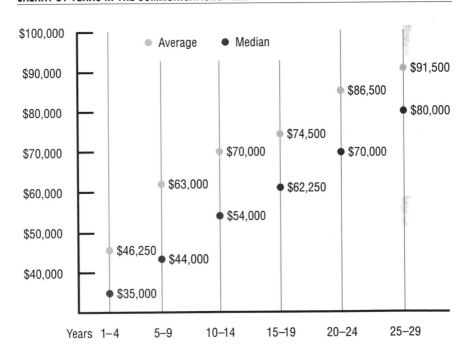

STRATEGIES FOR FINDING THE JOBS

There are an estimated 3.6 million active corporations in the United States. While not every one of them provides a setting in which communications majors would prefer to work, enough do.

Scan the Help-Wanted Ads

The traditional job-hunting method—reviewing help-wanted ads—seldom reaps rewards for the new, inexperienced grad. Most job advertisements are for specialists with time and experience under their belts or for pre-entry-level clerical jobs that might not offer enough exposure to lead to promotion. However, the want ads should not be ignored. The plum job you are perfect for could crop up in next Sunday's paper.

Knock on Doors

Knocking on doors is what experts advise. Find the firm for which you would like to work, and become a familiar face in the personnel department or front reception area.

Join Professional Associations

Professional associations often maintain job banks. The journals and newsletters they publish usually feature job advertisements. And the regional or national conferences they hold often have job clearinghouses with recruiters in attendance.

Find a Mentor

Your alumni association can put you in touch with professionals who might be able to give you leads.

Check with Your College Department

Don't forget to inquire at your communications department office. It is not unusual for a corporation to call a university and ask for a list of graduating seniors. The jobs they are seeking to fill might also be announced on department bulletin boards.

Register with Your College Placement Office

College placement offices and career service centers can also provide good leads for your job search. While some employers contact individual departments directly, others send their job openings to the placement office or career counselor.

HELP IN LOCATING THESE EMPLOYERS

Hit the library! Directories galore list professional associations, public relations firms, and corporations by industry. Make friends with your reference librarian and bring plenty of change for the copy machine.

The following contacts, journals, and directories only begin to scratch the surface.

Communication World
International Association of Business Communicators
One Hallidie Plaza, Ste. 600
San Francisco, CA 94102
www.iabc.com/homepage.htm

Encyclopedia of Associations
Gale Research, Inc.
P.O. Box 33477
Detroit, MI 48232

Foreign Service Recruitment Officer
Office of Personnel
United States Information Agency (USIA)
301 4th St. SW
Washington, DC 20547

O'Dwyer's Directory of Corporate Communications
O'Dwyer's Directory of Public Relations Firms
J.R. O'Dwyer Company, Inc.
271 Madison Ave.
New York, NY 10016

Investor Relations Newsletter
Enterprise Publications
20 N. Wacker Dr.
Chicago, IL 60606

Journal of Communication
Annenberg School Press
P.O. Box 13358
Philadelphia, PA 19101

Peace Corps Recruiting Office
1111 20th St., NW
Washington, DC 20526

PR Reporter
P.O. Box 600
Exeter, NH 03833

Public Relations Journal
Public Relations Career Opportunities
Public Relations Society of America
33 Irving Pl.
New York, NY 10003
www.prsa.org

Public Relations News
127 E. 80th St.
New York, NY 10021

Public Relations Quarterly
44 W. Market St.
Rhinebeck, NY 12572

Public Relations Review
7338 Baltimore Blvd., #101A
College Park, MD 20740

Speechwriter's Newsletter
Ragan Communications
407 S. Dearborn
Chicago, IL 60605

Training
50 S. 9th St.
Minneapolis, MN 55402

PROFESSIONAL ASSOCIATIONS

A glance through the list will show the variety of professional associations active in the world of business communications. Most offer booklets and pamphlets free of charge or for a nominal one or two dollar charge. Many of the associations listed provide job placement services and publish career-oriented journals and magazines. Visit their websites or drop them an E-mail or note for more information.

American Advertising Federation
Education Services Department
1101 Vermont Ave. NW, Ste. 500
Washington, DC 20005
www.aaf.org
Services: training, internships, conferences, awards, competitions

American Association of Advertising Agencies
405 Lexington Ave.
New York, NY 10174-1801
www.aaaa.org
Services: job locating, conferences, training

American Business Association
292 Madison Ave., 7th Floor
New York, NY 10017
Services: financial, publications

American Business Women's Association
9100 Ward Pkwy., P.O. Box 8728
Kansas City, MO 64114-0728
www.abwahq.org
Services: conferences, awards

American Society of Hospital Marketing and Public Relations
840 N. Lake Shore Dr.
Chicago, IL 60611
Services: annual conference, publications

American Society for Training and Development
Box 1443 1640 King St.
Alexandria, VA 22313
www.astd.org
Services: job bank, career information, training, seminars, workshops,
publications

Association for Business Communicators
Association for Business Communication
Box G-1326, Baruch College
17 Lexington Ave.
New York, NY 10010

www.theabc.org
Services: publications, conventions, awards

Associated Business Writers of America
1450 S. Havana, Ste. 424
Aurora, CO 80012
Services: publications

The Association for Women in Communications
780 Ritchie Hwy., Ste. 28S
Severna Park, MD 21146
www.womcom.org
Services: publications, annual conference, placement service, career information

Health Sciences Communications Association
One Wedgewood Dr., Ste. 28
Jewett City, CT 06351-2428
www.hesca.org
Services: annual conference, local and regional meetings, publications, job placement services

Institute for Public Relations
Research and Education
University of Florida
P.O. Box 118400
Gainesville, FL 32611-8400
www.instituteforpr.com
Services: research, annual lectures, competitions, publications

International Association of Business Communicators (IABC)
One Hallidie Plz., Ste. 600
San Francisco, CA 94102
www.iabc.com/homepage.htm
Services: career and job postings, publications, conferences

International Communication Association (ICA)
P.O. Box 9589
Austin, TX 78766
www.icahdq.org
Services: conferences, publications

International Labor Communications Association
815 16th St. NW, Rm. 509
Washington, DC 20006
Services: publications

The International Listening Association
www.listen.org
Services: conventions, publications

National Business Association
P.O. Box 700728
Dallas, TX 75370
www.nationalbusiness.org
Services: publications, scholarships

National Communication Association (NCA)
1765 N St. NW
Washington, DC 20036
www.natcom.org
Services: annual convention, conferences, publications, awards, job placement

National Council for Marketing and Public Relations
4602 W. 21st St. Circle
Greely, CO 80634
www.ncmpr.org
Services: annual conference, publications

Public Relations Society of America (PRSA)
33 Irving Pl.
New York, NY 10003-2376
www.prsa.org
Services: training, publications, job listings (in journal)

Religious Communication Association (RCA)
Weber State University
3750 Harrison Blvd.
Ogden, UT 84408
http://gcc.bradley.edu/com/faculty/lamoureux/rsca/index.html
Services: conferences, workshops, seminars, publications

Sales and Marketing Executives International
P.O. Box 1390
Sumas, WA 98295-1390
www.smei.org
Services: job listings, conferences, training, publications, business services

CHAPTER ELEVEN

PATH 2: CONSUMER COMMUNICATIONS

 hile corporate communicators and PR professionals aim their communications at varying publics, specialists in this career path concern themselves solely with the consumer, the customer.

Because we have progressed from an agrarian way of life to a complex society filled with commercial activity, competing for the consumer dollar has become a necessity for business survival and economic well-being in general.

We are a country of choices. Just go into any American supermarket and walk down the cereal or soap aisles. How many ways can we start off our mornings or wash our clothes, dishes, floors, and bodies? Some would say too many, but that's not the point. In a free enterprise system, competition is the name of the game, and to succeed or just stay afloat, businesses have to attract the consumer with the biggest, tastiest, most colorful, most convenient, most healthful, and most efficient product or service.

Like it or not, methods of reaching the consumer and getting a share of that dollar have permeated every aspect of our lives. Advertising is all around us, through print, film, broadcasting, public appearances, and a host of other devices and campaigns.

Consumers might sometimes see this bombardment as an intrusion; for communications majors, it has opened the door to a wide range of employment possibilities.

DEFINITION OF THE CAREER PATH

While some of the careers explored in this chapter are entered by graduates with field-specific majors (advertising majors going into advertising, marketing majors going into marketing, and so forth), graduates of communications programs are blazing new trails as well as following well-established ones through a variety of terrains. University communications departments now cover areas that once belonged to different and separate departments. They offer programs that successfully compete with departments of business, advertising, marketing, public relations, journalism, broadcasting, and a host of other fields.

The skills students acquire ignore career boundaries that these days are becoming more and more ill-defined. Not wanting to limit the potential talent they could attract, many employers and personnel directors shy away from specifying particular majors when advertising an opening. While bachelor's degrees still continue to be at least the minimum requirement, and increasing competition makes a master's degree even more desirable, the designated major is not as important.

Here is a sample job advertisement within this career path that stresses skills and responsibilities rather than majors.

ACCOUNT EXECUTIVE

Expanding advertising agency seeks customer-service-oriented professional to provide strategic guidance and advertising expertise to a growing list of clients. Minimum requirements: bachelor's degree and three years experience as a human resource generalist. Must have ability to establish and maintain long-standing relationships with major corporate clients, work independently, listen, and analyze client needs. Outgoing, poised individual with strong communication skills a must. Send resume to . . .

Not only is a major not specified in the sample ad, but the employer is seeking a generalist, someone who has not been pigeonholed by his or her work experience or university program. If you isolate the required skills mentioned, you will see that they could all belong to a communications major.

Advertising and Marketing

Although advertising and marketing are distinct fields, they are often linked together. Some definitions peg marketing as the broad category that encompasses advertising as well as disciplines such as public relations and sales. In simple terms, advertisers create a package to sell a product, service, or idea; marketing experts help decide toward which audiences the advertisement should be aimed.

The goal of advertising and marketing is to reach the consumer—to motivate or persuade a potential buyer; to sell a product, service, idea, or cause; to gain political support; or to influence public opinion. In the words of the American Association of Advertising Agencies (known as the 4 As):

Advertising is an indispensable part of our economic system. It is the vital link between businesses and consumers.

The business of advertising involves marketing objectives and artistic ingenuity. It applies quantitative and qualitative research to the creative process. It is the marriage of analysis and imagination, of marketing professional and artist.

Advertising is art and science, show business and just plain business, all rolled into one. And it employs some of the brightest and most creative economists, researchers, artists, producers, writers, and business people in the country today.

To aid in the advertising endeavor, marketing professionals gather public opinion or analyze the demographics and buying patterns of specific audiences. They play the role of researcher, statistician, social psychologist, and sociologist.

With the specific target audience in mind, advertising professionals assess the competition, set goals and a budget, design an advertisement—whether a simple three-line ad or a full-blown campaign—and determine how to best bring their message to that audience.

Most advertising agencies are organized into the following departments (although within smaller agencies, departments can be combined or services contracted out to independent subcontractors): agency management, account management,creative services, traffic control and production, media services, publicity and public relations, sales promotion, direct response, television production, and personnel.

To work within these departments, advertising agencies employ a number of professionals to perform a variety of duties.

Agency Manager. In a small agency, the manager might be the president, owner, or a partner. In giant agencies, the manager might be the chief executive officer reporting to a board of directors or an executive committee, in much the same way any corporation functions

The agency manager is responsible for establishing policies and planning, developing, and defining goals to ensure growth and economic viability.

Account Manager/Executive. An agency's client is usually called an account. The account manager supervises all the activity involved with a specific account and is ultimately responsible for the quality of service the client receives.

The account manager functions as a liaison between the advertising agency and the client's organization. He or she must be thoroughly familiar with the client's business, the consumer, the marketplace, and all the aspects of advertising, such as media, research, creative design, and commercial production.

Small agencies might function with just one account manager; large megaagencies could have hundreds or thousands, each handling a multitude of accounts.

Account managers usually reach their position after working up through the ranks.

Assistant Account Manager/Executive. Commonly, the assistant account manager reports directly to an account manager and can be assigned a wide range of duties. Some of these include analyzing the competition, writing reports, and coordinating creative, media, production, and research projects.

Candidates should possess at least a bachelor's degree, but a specific major in advertising or marketing is not a prerequisite, and communications majors are highly regarded.

Account management departments, along with media departments, hire the greatest number of entry-level candidates. Entry-level positions within the field of advertising can rapidly lead to more senior roles.

Creative/Art Director. The creative department of an advertising agency develops the ideas, images, words, and methods that contribute to the ultimate product: the commercial, ad, or campaign. Within an agency's creative department, many different professionals work together to meet the needs of the client. The art director works with writers, artists, and producers, from the conception of the advertisement to its final production.

Entry into the creative department of an advertising agency, as a copywriter, designer, or assistant art director, is particularly competitive. Having a good portfolio to present to the art director will be a plus, and submitting freelance work can also help you get a foot in the door.

Assistant/Junior Art Director. The assistant art director reports to one or more art directors and is commonly responsible for preparing paste-ups and layouts for television storyboards and print ads. The assistant can also be involved in developing visual concepts and designs, and, supervising commercial production and photo sessions.

Employers expect job candidates to have at least a two-year associate's degree from an art or design school but also appreciate bachelor's-level communications majors with strong graphic arts experience. Even more important is being able to show a top-quality portfolio that displays skill and creativity.

The American Association of Advertising Agencies reports that entry-level opportunities in art departments are very limited for those without some related business experience, such as an internship or practicum spent in a retail advertising department or some other related setting.

Copywriter and Assistant/Junior Copywriter. Copywriters write body copy for print advertising and develop sales promotional materials. Assignments range from creating names for companies and products or writing television commercial dialogue, scripts for radio spots, or copy for direct mail packages. Junior copywriters assist the copywriter and also edit and proofread.

Although a bachelor's degree is not required—a strong portfolio could beat out a degree holder—majors that are sought after include communications, English, journalism, advertising, and marketing. Even though some of the largest advertising agencies offer copywriting training programs, opportunities are limited for those with no writing experience.

Print Production Managers and Assistants. The print production department of an agency is responsible for the final creation of the advertisement. After the creative team has specified the different elements that must be incorporated into an ad, the print production team sees that the instructions are carried through. They are responsible for two-color, four-color, and black and white printing, color separations, and the preparation of mechanicals.

The print production department works closely with the traffic department and the creative staff and is also responsible for quality control.

Some experience with production work is usually required to enter this department. Although not the most competitive area, it is still a good place for someone to break in, and move up.

Assistant Media Planner. The media department is responsible for making sure the advertising is presented to the right audiences, at the right time, and at the right place. As mentioned earlier, media departments are usually open to hiring entry-level candidates.

The assistant media planner reports to a senior planner. His or her usual duties are as follows:

Gather and study information about people's viewing and reading habits.

Evaluate programming and editorial content of different media vehicles.

Calculate reach and frequency for specific target groups and campaigns.

Become completely familiar with the media in general.

Become completely familiar with specific media outlets.

Become completely familiar with media banks and information and research sources.

Media Buyer. Media buyers and their assistants keep track of where and when print space and air time are available for purchase. They verify that agency orders actually appear or run and calculate costs and rates. They are familiar with all media outlets and are skilled at negotiations.

Media buyers also possess the ability to work under pressure, excellent communications skills, and strong general business skills. They are also adept at working with numbers and are familiar with basic computer programs such as spreadsheet software.

Candidates for entry-level positions are expected to have earned a four-year degree. Some of the large agencies offer training programs for new hires.

Traffic Managers and Assistants. People working in the traffic department make sure that the various projects are conceived, produced, and placed as specified. This department is in charge of scheduling and record keeping. The traffic department is an excellent place for those with more interest than experience to get a foothold.

Market Research. Professionals working in market research departments are tuned in to the consumer—what he or she worries about, desires, thinks, believes, and holds dear. Market researchers conduct surveys or one-on-one interviews, use existing research, test consumer reactions to new products or advertising copy, track sales figures and buying trends, and become overall experts on consumer behavior.

Agency research departments design questionnaires or other methods of studying groups of people, implement the surveys, and interpret the results. Sometimes, research departments hire an outside market research firm to take over some of the workload. For example, a market researcher could come up with a procedure to test the public's reaction to a television commercial; the outside firm puts the procedure into action.

Assistant Research Executive. Assistants report directly to a research executive and are responsible for compiling and interpreting data and monitoring the progress of research projects.

An entry-level assistant research executive has strong quantitative skills and a good aptitude for analyzing data. In addition, they must have computer skills and the ability to write and speak effectively.

In this field a bachelor's degree is the basic requirement, but it is becoming more and more common to find master's and Ph.D. holders. A graduate of a college program that emphasizes research will have an edge over the competition.

Publicity and Promotion

While advertising is written exactly the way the client wants and is placed where he or she hopes it will have the most impact, publicity—its wording and placement—is determined by the staff of the media to which it is sent. All the media outlets (covered in Chapter 12) have the option to rewrite press releases or even ignore them. When used properly, however, publicity provides free advertising for products, services, and events.

When it comes to promotion, the clients or business owners have more control. They stage events, organize activities, and print and distribute promotional materials.

Here are a few examples of the way publicity and promotion work:

A sports figure endorses a brand of athletic shoe (for a fee, of course).

A television talk show host invites the author of a new book to be a guest on the program.

A publisher arranges a book-signing tour to promote an author's new book.

A model demonstrates the features of a yacht at a boat show.

A soap opera star signs autographs on a tour of shopping malls.

A professional association imprints its name and logo on tote bags to be given away at the annual conference.

A political candidate reads a ghostwritten speech at a rally.

A television magazine format show explores a breakthrough cure for cancer.

A vacation resort entices travel writers to visit.

Budweiser sponsors a "BeerFest" at a sporting event.

A "guerrilla marketer" stands on the street corner and thrusts free samples of a product into the hands of passersby.

Someone wearing a Big Bird outfit stands in front of a shop, inviting passersby to enter.

Those in charge of organizing these promotional activities are sometimes called publicists as well as PR people. They work in a variety of settings and have a wide range of duties. The most important thing they have in common is that they are all excellent communicators. They are also creative people with extensive knowledge of and contact with the media.

POSSIBLE JOB TITLES

A wide variety of job titles is associated with consumer communications careers. In addition, within certain job titles there are different rankings. For example, the position of account executive would have as entry-level positions the assistant account executive or junior account executive; the next rank up would be associate account executive, moving on to senior account executive and account manager.

This list will give you an idea of the jobs available. You will be able to add to the list as you investigate all the possibilities.

Account coordinator	Market research manager
Account director	Media buyer
Account/district manager	Media director
Account executive	Media evaluator
Account representative	Media placement specialist
Account specialist	Media planner
Account supervisor	Media supervisor
Account trainee	Print production manager
Advertising director	Producer
Art buyer	Production assistant
Art director	Production manager
Broadcast production manager	Project director
Consumer affairs specialist	Promotion manager
Copyeditor	Publicist
Copywriter	Research assistant
Creative director	Researcher
Designer	Sales assistant
Editor	Sales planner
Event coordinator	Sales representative
Graphic artist	Spokesperson
Management supervisor	Traffic assistant
Market analyst	Traffic manager

POSSIBLE EMPLOYERS

Advertising Agencies

There are more than 21,000 advertising establishments in the United States, employing more than 268,000 workers. About six out of ten write copy and prepare artwork, graphics, and other creative work and then place the resulting ads in periodicals, newspapers, radio, television, or other advertising media. Within the industry, only these full-service establishments are known as advertising agencies. Many of the largest agencies are international, with a substantial proportion of their revenue coming from abroad.

About three out of ten advertising firms specialize in a particular market niche. Some companies produce and solicit outdoor advertising, such as billboards and electric displays. Buses, subways, taxis, airports, and bus terminals also frequently carry ads. A small number of firms produce aerial advertising, while others distribute circulars, handbills, and free samples.

Groups within agencies have been created to serve their clients' electronic advertising needs on the Internet. The Internet is a medium that fosters rapid growth of advertising and commercial activities. Advertisements often link users from one website to the company's or product's website where information such as new product announcements, contests, and product catalogs appear.

Some firms are not involved in the creation of ads at all; instead, they sell advertising time or space on radio and television stations or in publications. Because these firms do not produce advertising, their staffs are mostly sales workers.

In an effort to attract and maintain clients, advertising agencies are diversifying their services, offering advertising as well as sales, marketing, public relations, and interactive media services.

Advertising firms have found that highly creative work is particularly suitable for outsourcing, resulting in a better product and increasing the firm's profitability.

Although advertising firms are located throughout the country, they are concentrated in the largest cities: New York with the most firms, Chicago, and Los Angeles. Other top cities are Detroit, San Francisco, Minneapolis, Boston, and Dallas. Firms vary in size, ranging from one-person shops to international agencies employing thousands of workers.

About four of five advertising firms employ fewer than ten employees. The small size of the average advertising firm demonstrates the opportunities for self-employment. It is relatively easy to open a small ad agency; in fact, many successful agencies began as one- or two-person operations. Approximately 15 percent of all advertising workers are self-employed, compared to 9 percent of workers in all industries combined.

Marketing Firms/Departments

Marketers and advertising professionals work hand in hand, and thus many marketing departments are located within corporate advertising departments or within private advertising agencies. Private marketing firms function similarly to advertising agencies and work toward the same goals: identifying and targeting specific audiences that will be receptive to specific products, services, or ideas.

Corporate Advertising Departments

While many companies use the services of outside advertising agencies and marketing firms, just as many, especially the very large ones, operate their own in-house departments. Here, workers create and develop the company's advertising and sales promotion material. For example, a large department store, such as Macy's or Bloomingdale's, will have its professional staff create catalogs, brochures, newspaper inserts, flyers, as well as place the regular flow of daily newspaper ads.

Developing this material, especially glossy catalogs, is a big endeavor, requiring the skills of a variety of people. Copywriters, art directors, photographers, layout artists, and modeling agencies and models all play a part.

Corporations that use the services of an outside agency might also maintain their own advertising department to function as a liaison between the agency and the company. Here the responsibilities include ensuring that the advertising being produced meets the company's objectives and is placed in the appropriate media outlets.

Self-Employed/Freelancers

Freelancers offer their services to advertising agencies and corporations. They are usually looked to when staffing is not sufficient to handle a new client or there is a sudden overload of work. Freelancers also have successful working relationships with small businesses that don't have the desire or budget to work with a large, expensive agency.

Freelancers can pick and choose their projects, although starting out that way is usually not an option. Once established, though, a freelancer who finds himself with enough clients can open his own office. As the client load increases, so does the need to have help, and this is how many small agencies get their start—an enterprising freelancer builds up enough business to take on employees.

Freelance publicists work with people who, simply put, need publicity. Here are some examples. An author with a self-published book he needs to promote wants to get booked on radio or television talk shows or at bookstores for booksignings. A former politician wants to get on the university campus speaker circuit. An independent film company with a small-time budget wants a chance at big-time distribution.

Publishing Companies

Large publishing companies, especially those located in New York City, operate publicity departments to promote their authors and their books. Some of the duties of a publishing house publicist are: arranging for point-of-sale material (for example, printed bookmarks) to be made available at bookstores; organizing book tours, including booking speaking engagements on television and radio shows and setting up book-signing engagements at bookstores and other appropriate outlets; and writing book jacket copy.

Bookstores

More and more bookstores, especially the new superstores, coordinate events to bring in the customers. This calls for a publicist who can book national and local authors for speaking and signing engagements; arrange for cookbook authors to give demonstrations; and find other ways to appeal to the tastes of the book-buying public.

Vacation Resorts/Chambers of Commerce

Promoting a vacation spot or city falls into the realm of a publicist's duties. Publicists working for a vacation resort produce pamphlets, brochures, press releases, and even video demonstrations of the location's selling points. Their target audience consists of travel agents, travel writers and editors, and the vacationing public.

Publicists working for chambers of commerce aim their efforts at potential businesses and new residents as well as vacationers and other visitors.

Other settings where this career path can be followed (for example, government agencies, nonprofit associations, educational institutions, and health care facilities) are covered in Chapter 10.

RELATED OCCUPATIONS

The skills used by communications majors in advertising, marketing, publicity, and promotion can also be transferred to different settings. A market analyst, for example, who is adept at collecting and interpreting data on different populations, could also work for the government as a demographer helping to prepare a census or with an insurance company as an actuarian.

Advertising photography	Convention sales
Travel photography	Demographer
Fund-raiser	Actuarian
Membership services director	Statistician
Function sales manager	Campaign developer
Hotel Sales	Researcher

WORKING CONDITIONS

The field of consumer communications is a competitive business, with every industry vying for the all-important consumer dollar. While this can make the working atmosphere challenging and exciting, it can also make it hectic and stressful.

A busy ad agency, for example, will have a long list of ongoing projects that need attention at the same time. No matter how large the agency may be or how many professionals it employs, in some agencies the workload strains available staff. This atmosphere lends itself to employees feeling overworked. It is not uncommon for burnout to occur after a few years of constant pressure.

In order to attract clients and beat out the competition, there are campaigns to be developed and ideas and concepts to be presented. If the account managers misjudge the goals of the client, there's the stress of losing an account. If the campaign is successful, there are still pressures to keep that client—not to mention the deadlines to be met and the crises to be resolved when things go wrong.

Hours can be long and disruptive to a personal life. Contributing to this is a substantial amount of travel—to meet with clients or attend conferences—that managers for some agencies might have to do.

Although the life of an ad exec might seem "glamorous" to many, the reality is that the work is less secure than most, with staff layoffs occurring when the workload drops.

TRAINING AND QUALIFICATIONS

The course of study a potential consumer communications specialist should pursue has been the issue of some debate. Some believe that a straight degree in advertising is the best preparation, but they are usually shouted down by those who recognize the importance of a broader curriculum.

To some extent, the answer is determined by the area of the career path you intend to pursue. If you are aiming for a title of account manager, then courses in marketing, business and finance, and speech communications are as important as advertising theory. Potential art directors obviously need technical training in drawing, illustration, and graphic design. All are well served, however, by courses in effective communications.

In addition, have another look at the training and qualification requirements highlighted in Chapter 10. They all apply in this career path as well.

CAREER OUTLOOK

There are more than 21,000 advertising agencies in the United States, but the American Association of Advertising Agencies (the 4 As) estimates that the number of openings for new grads is only a fraction of that each year.

Marketing, advertising, and public relations managers hold about 485,000 jobs in the United States in virtually every industry. Employment is expected to increase faster than the average for all occupations through the year 2008. According to the *Occupational Outlook Handbook*, increasingly intense domestic and global competition in products and services offered to consumers should require greater marketing, advertising, public relations, and promotional efforts. As businesses increasingly hire contractors for these services, rather than support additional full-time staff, private consulting firms and agencies may experience particularly rapid growth.

Employment growth may be tempered by the increased use of more efficient technologies that could replace some workers. Competition for jobs will be keen because the glamour of the industry traditionally attracts many more job seekers than there are job openings. Employment also may be adversely affected if legislation further restricts advertising for specific products, such as alcoholic beverages, or via specific media, such as billboards.

EARNINGS

According to the U.S. Bureau of Labor Statistics, median annual earnings of advertising and marketing managers are approximately $57,300. The middle 50 percent earn between $38,230 and $84,950 a year. The lowest 10 percent earn less than $28,190 and the highest 10 percent earn more than $116,160 a year.

Median annual earnings in the industries employing the largest number of advertising and marketing managers are as follows:

Professional and commercial equipment	$69,800
Telephone communications	$64,100
Computer and data processing services	$60,800
Advertising	$54,300
Management and public relations	$51,100

According to a National Association of Colleges and Employers survey, starting salaries for marketing majors graduating in 1999 averaged about $31,900; advertising majors, about $26,600.

Salary levels vary substantially depending upon the level of managerial responsibility, length of service, education, firm size, location, and industry. For example, manufacturing firms usually pay advertising, marketing, and public relations managers higher salaries than nonmanufacturing firms do.

For sales managers, the size of their sales territory is another important determinant of salary. Many managers earn bonuses equal to 10 percent or more of their salaries.

Nonsupervisory workers in advertising average $647 a week—significantly higher than the $442 a week for all nonsupervisory workers in private industry.

The table below shows the median hourly earnings of the largest occupations in advertising, compared to all industries:

OCCUPATION	ADVERTISING	ALL INDUSTRIES
General managers and top executives	$45.53	$26.05
Marketing, advertising, and public relations managers	26.11	25.61
Writers and editors	18.31	15.69
Artists and related workers	16.74	14.89
Sales agents, advertising	15.68	14.16
First-line supervisors and managers /supervisors of clerical and administrative support workers	15.17	14.26
Secretaries, except legal and medical	11.89	11.00
Bookkeeping, accounting, and auditing clerks	11.54	10.80
General office clerks	9.23	9.10
Demonstrators and promoters	7.95	7.65

Other surveys show a variation of $25,000 to $250,000 for marketing managers, depending on the level of education, experience, industry, and the number of employees he or she supervises.

Salaries for sales professionals are harder to pin down. Depending upon the setting and the product, workers can earn as low as minimum wage or in the high six figures with commissions and bonuses figured in.

STRATEGIES FOR FINDING THE JOBS

As with the corporate world, it's a good idea for a job seeker to become a familiar fixture inside an advertising agency's front reception area. Sending out resumes blindly has never been the most effective method for finding a job in any profession. It works even less in these settings. The key is having a good portfolio with you, one that you can quickly open and display if the right person walks by. A portfolio should showcase your best work. If you are interested in copywriting, visuals are less important than writing samples and a good marketing sense. Aspiring art directors need samples of their work that show their design ability.

Persistence is a trait valued in this career path; showing the same quality in your job search can help pay off.

The strategies mentioned in Chapter 10 also apply here. Use your university's resources as well as the library's.

Here are some additional tips:

Start your job search before you near graduation. Those who arrange internships for themselves have an edge; they've already become familiar faces on-the-job. When an opening comes up a known commodity (who performed well during the internship) is going to be chosen over an unknown one.

Learn as much as you can about the agency or firm you're interested in. In other words, target your prospects.

HELP IN LOCATING THESE EMPLOYERS

The following list includes contacts, journals, and directories that can aid in your job search. Many of the publications are available as reference material.

Adweek
Adweek Online
Brandweek
Mediaweek
770 Broadway, 7th Fl.
New York, NY 10003
www.adweek.com

Advertising Age
Crain Communications, Inc.
711 Third Ave.
New York, NY 10017-4036
www.adage.com

Advertising Career Directory
Magazine Publishing Career Directory
Public Relations Career Directory
Gale Research, Inc.
P.O. Box 33477
Detroit, MI 48232-5477

Encyclopedia of Associations
Gale Research, Inc.
P.O. Box 33477
Detroit, MI 48232

Standard Directory of Advertisers (The Advertiser Red Book)
Standard Directory of Advertising Agencies (The Agency Red Book)
Reed Reference Publishing
P.O. Box 31
New Providence, NJ 07974
The Agency Red Book lists more than four thousand agencies and includes regional offices, accounts specializations, number of employees, and names and titles of key personnel. It is published every February, June, and October.

U.S. Department of Commerce
Maintains a list of approximately eight thousand advertising agencies nationwide.

PROFESSIONAL ASSOCIATIONS

The following list of professional associations will give you an idea of the variety available within this career path. Receiving detailed information about each association and the professional area it supports takes only a letter or phone call.

The Advertising Club of New York
235 Park Ave. S, 6th Fl.
New York, NY 10003
www.andyawards.com
Services: annual advertising and marketing course with classes in copywriting, special graphics, verbal communication, advertising production, and others; publications, membership directory

Advertising Council
261 Madison Ave.
New York, NY 10016-2303
Services: conducts public service advertising campaigns, publications

Advertising Photographers of America, Inc.
27 W. 20th St.
New York, NY 10011
Services: lectures, seminars, discussion groups, publications

Advertising Research Foundation
641 Lexington Ave.
New York, NY 10022
www.arfsite.org
Services: annual meeting, regional meetings, workshops, conferences, publications

Advertising Women of New York
153 E. 57th St.
New York, NY 10022
Services: annual career conference for college seniors, publications, job listings

American Advertising Federation
Education Services Department
1101 Vermont Ave. NW, Ste. 500

Washington, DC 20005
www.aaf.org
Services: training, internships, conferences, awards, competitions

American Association of Advertising Agencies
405 Lexington Ave.
New York, NY 10174-1801
www.aaaa.org
Services: job locating, conferences, training

American Council of Highway Advertisers
P.O. Box 809
North Beach, MD 20714
www.penrose-press.com/IDD/org/cards/S3452.html

American Marketing Association
311 S. Wacker Dr., Ste. 5800
Chicago, IL 60606
www.ama.org
Services: seminars, conferences, student marketing clubs, placement service,
publications

Association of National Advertisers
708 Third Ave.
New York, NY 10017-4270
www.ana.net
Services: conducts studies, surveys, seminars, and workshops, and provides
a specialized education program, publishes *The Advertiser*

Council of Sales Promotion Agencies
750 Summer St.
Stamford, CT 06901
Services: intern program, conducts research

National Council for Marketing and Public Relations
4602 W. 21st St. Circle
Greeley, CO 80634
www.ncmpr.org
Services: annual conference, national surveys, needs assessment, awards,
publications

Point of Purchase Advertising International
1600 L St. NW, 10th Fl.
Washington, DC 20036
www.popai.com
Services: conducts student education programs, publications

Retail Advertising & Marketing Association
333 N. Michigan Ave., Ste. 3000
Chicago, IL 60601
www.penrose-press.com/IDD/org/cards/S3453.html

Sales and Marketing Executives International
P.O. Box 1390
Sumas, WA 98295-1390
www.smei.org
Services: job listings, conferences, training, publications, business services

Specialty Advertising Association International
3125 Skyway Circle N
Irving, TX 75038-3526
Services: speakers bureau, conducts research, and organizes executive training and development seminars, publications

CHAPTER TWELVE

PATH 3: MEDIA

In the previous chapters we have explored getting the corporate word out to a variety of publics, and getting the advertising word out to consumers.

In this chapter, we are not so narrowly focused; we can look at all the other words people strive to get out and the outlets they use to do so. But this career path should not be viewed as a rain barrel of excess categories, the catchall of the communications field. The media and all it encompasses is perhaps the most vital system for communication in a free enterprise system and democracy.

Here, the messages are broad and far-reaching, the goals as varied as the professionals who work in the different fields. Loosely defined, the media is any outlet that lets us get the word out; and the word we get out enables our audiences to be informed, educated, and entertained.

The United States supports the largest mass media system of any country in the world, which in turn has generated millions of jobs. The choices for communications majors in search of great jobs could almost be daunting if it weren't so exciting.

The field of journalism is perhaps the most traditional path open to communications majors, but no longer does the fourth estate refer only to newspapers. It includes syndicates and wire services, television and radio, and consumer and trade publications. And while these outlets provide a home for journalists to report and interpret the news, they also furnish niches for creative writers with a vast array of specialties, as well as important front-line and support positions for editors, agents, entertainers, broadcasters, producers, photographers, computer experts, and others.

Communications majors can plan ahead while in school, taking courses and honing the skills that will allow them to work in any number of media outlets. While many of the skills needed are field specific, many others can be transferred for use from one sector of the media to another.

DEFINITION OF THE CAREER PATH

Because there is such a vast range of jobs within the media, and many of the same positions are found in several different outlets, it is more efficient here to examine each outlet as a career path unto itself. While the role of editor, for example, will vary to some degree depending upon the setting, many of the same functions are performed and the same skills used in newspapers as well as magazines. The definitive question is not whether to become an editor, but which milieu would best suit the future editor.

Similarly, a communications major with hopes of becoming a writer will benefit from knowing the types of assignments and working conditions involved at the different job settings, or whether a career as a freelancer is a viable alternative.

For every interest a communications major has, there is a job and a setting to satisfy it.

POSSIBLE JOB TITLES

Job titles within the media run the gamut from writers and editors to entertainers production people, and a host of other professionals working in departments not covered in this chapter. This list is not meant to be exhaustive. You will find additional related job tides and descriptions in other chapters of this book; *The Dictionary of Occupational Titles* (U.S. Department of Labor) gives a comprehensive list with generic descriptions.

PRINT MEDIA

Acquisitions editor	City editor
Art director	Columnist
Assignment editor	Contracts assistant
Assistant editor	Copyeditor
Associate editor	Copywriter
Author	Correspondent
Book editor	Critic
Bureau chief	Desk assistant
Bureau reporter	Dramatic agent

Editor
Editorial Assistant
Editorial writer
Editor in chief
Electronic publishing specialist
Executive editor
External publications editor
Feature writer
Freelance editor
Freelance writer
International publications editor
Investigative reporter
Journalist
Literary agent
Managing editor
News editor
Newspaper editor

News writer
Photojournalist
President
Production editor
Publisher
Reporter
Researcher
Section editor
Senior editor
Senior writer
Staff writer
Story editor
Stringer
Syndicated columnist
Technical editor
Wire editor
Writer

RADIO, TELEVISION, AND MULTIMEDIA

Announcer
Associate news director
AV manager/director
AV producer
AV technician
AV writer
Broadcast engineer
Broadcast technician
CAD specialist
Correspondent
Director
Disc jockey
Filmmaker
First assistant director
Graphics coordinator
Media resource director
Mixer
Music Director
Music librarian
Newscaster

News announcer
News director
News editor
News writer
Operations manager
Production assistant
Production manager
Production sound mixer
Program manager
Public services director
Radio/TV traffic assistant
Radio/TV traffic supervisor
Scriptwriter
Station manager
TV director
TV managing editor
TV producer
TV production assistant
TV tape-film manager
Video specialist

NEWSPAPERS

Current figures show that there are approximately 9,200 newspapers in the United States; 1,700 are dailies, most of which are evening newspapers, and the remainder are weeklies. The number of major dailies has declined in recent years; there are only about 35 newspapers with a circulation of more than 250,000. Despite declining numbers, newspapers rank as the third largest industry in the United States and employ 450,000 people.

Newspapers are usually organized around the following departments: news, editorial, advertising, production, and circulation. All provide job opportunities for communications majors. For the purpose of this chapter, we will focus on the news and editorial sections.

The News Department

Within the news section we will examine careers for reporters and photojournalists.

Reporters. A job as a reporter is viewed as a glamorous and exciting type of existence, summoning up images of Clark Kent and Lois Lane, and probably attracts more applicants than any other spot on a newspaper staff. As a result, competition is stiff; reporters make up less than one-fourth of a newspaper's roster.

Reporting work is challenging and fast paced, with the pressures of deadlines and space allotments always looming over head. It's the ideal job for those who like to be one step ahead of the general public in knowing what's going on.

Whatever the size or location of the newspaper, the job of a reporter is to cover local, state, national, and international events and put all this news together to keep the reading public informed. News reporters can be assigned to a variety of stories, from covering a major world event, monitoring the actions of public figures, or writing about a current political campaign.

Photojournalists. Photojournalism is telling a story through pictures. And though it's a form of journalism in which photographs dominate over written copy, photojournalists need to have a strong journalism background. To accurately report the news, whether through photographs or copy, you need to be aware of what's happening in the world and why.

Being a jack-of-all-trades is the main requirement. Most photojournalists, whether working for a major or a minor newspaper, are expected to cover the exciting as well as the tame. Their assignments run from food to fashion, from spot news to sports to a wide range of human interest features.

The Editorial Department

The editorial sections within newspapers vary with size and location but most include at least some, if not all of, the following sections:

Art	Health
Business	International news
Books	Lifestyles/features
Consumer affairs	Local news
The courts	National news
Crime desk	Religion
Education	Science
Entertainment	Social events
Fashion	Sports
Finance	State news
Food	Travel
Foreign affairs	Weather

Within the editorial department we will look at the key positions of staff writers and section editors.

Staff Writers. Staff or feature writers function in much the same way as news reporters, but are generally assigned a regular "beat," such as health and medicine, sports, travel, or consumer affairs. Working in these specialized fields, staff writers keep the public informed about important trends or breakthroughs in a variety of areas.

Contrary to some misconceived notions, feature writers are not assigned only fluff pieces. While a fashion writer might not do in-depth investigative pieces, a health and medicine writer often will. Nancy McVicar, for example, is a senior writer at the *Sun-Sentinel*, a newspaper with a circulation of about one million in Fort Lauderdale, Florida. She works for the Lifestyle section, which has a health page every Thursday, and her work has been nominated for the Pulitzer Prize seven times. Several of her stories have won other prestigious national awards.

McVicar was the first to break the story on the safety issues related to cellular telephones. Her articles on the topic went out over the wire and also ended up on the television news shows "20/20" and "60 Minutes." The GAO (the General Accounting Office of the U.S. Government, which is also the investigative arm of Congress) was asked to do an in-depth report on whether or not cellular phones are safe, based on McVicar's stories.

Writers in every section of a newspaper can find a way to make an impact.

Section Editors. A job as a section editor is considered by many to be a plum position. Although there are exceptions, section editors have usually paid their dues as reporters or staff writers.

The duties involved depend in part on the section, but there are many responsibilities in common. Editors write articles or supervise the work of staff writers, making assignments, reviewing copy, and making sure attention is paid to space requirements. They also attend editorial meetings and correspond with freelance writers.

Many perks are associated with some of the sections; travel writers get to travel, book editors get free books in the mail to read and review, sports editors get to go to a lot of the games, food editors get to eat, society page editors get invited to myriad social events, and so on.

Working Conditions

Reporters and photojournalists always have deadlines hanging over their heads. Unlike fiction writers, who can work at their own pace, reporters do not have the luxury of waiting for their creative juices to begin to flow. A news reporter has to file a story, or maybe even two, every day by a certain time. A staff writer or section editor with a weekly column has more leeway, but everything must still be in by press time.

Reporters gather information by visiting the scene, interviewing people, following leads and news tips, and examining documents. While some reporters might rely on their memory, most take notes or use a tape recorder while collecting facts. Back. in the office, they organize their material, decide what the focus or emphasis should be, and then write their stories, generally using a computer. Because of deadlines, while away from the office many reporters use portable computers to file the story, which is then sent by telephone modem directly to the newspaper's computer system.

Some newspapers have modern, state-of-the-art equipment; others do not have the financing they need to update. A reporter might work in a comfortable, private office, or in a room filled with the noise of computer printers and coworkers talking on the telephone.

Working hours vary. Some writers and editors work Monday through Friday, nine to five, while others cover evenings, nights, and weekends.

On some occasions, reporters work longer than normal hours to cover an important ongoing story or to follow late-breaking developments.

Although some desk work is involved, newspaper reporting is definitely not a desk job. Reporters must have excellent interviewing and research skills and the ability to juggle several assignments at once. Computer and typing skills are very important, too.

A reporter also must know how to write tight. While feature writers can be more creative, news reporters must make sure they get all the facts in within a certain amount of space. The editor might allocate only a column inch or two for your story, leaving room for just the who, what, when, where, why, and how.

Training and Qualifications

A college degree is a must; most employers prefer a B.A. in journalism or communications, while others accept a degree in a related field such as political science or English.

The courses you should take in college include introductory mass media, basic reporting and copyediting, history of journalism, and press law and ethics.

Previous work on a school paper or an internship at a newspaper will help to enhance your resume. Experience as a stringer—a part-time reporter who is paid only for stories printed—is also helpful.

Photojournalism is highly competitive, so having a good portfolio is very important. Most photojournalists have at least a bachelor's degree, many, especially those with management inclinations, have a master's.

Career Outlook

Overall employment of news analysts, reporters, and correspondents is expected to grow little through the year 2008—the result of mergers, consolidations, and closures of newspapers; decreased circulation; increased expenses; and a decline in advertising profits. In spite of little change in overall employment, some job growth is expected in radio and television stations, whereas more rapid growth is expected in new media areas, such as on-line newspapers and magazines.

Competition will continue to be keen for jobs on large metropolitan newspapers and broadcast stations and on national magazines. Talented writers who can handle highly specialized scientific or technical subjects have an advantage. Also, more newspapers than ever before are hiring stringers and freelancers.

Most entry-level openings arise on small publications, as reporters and correspondents become editors or reporters on larger publications or leave the field. Small-town and suburban newspapers will continue to offer the most opportunities for persons seeking to enter this field.

Turnover is relatively high in this occupation. Some find the work too stressful and hectic or do not like the lifestyle and transfer to other occupations. Journalism graduates have the background for work in closely related fields such as advertising and public relations, and many take jobs in these fields. Other graduates accept sales, managerial, or other nonmedia positions, because of the difficulty in finding media jobs.

The newspaper and broadcasting industries are sensitive to economic ups and downs because these industries depend on advertising revenue. During recessions, few new reporters are hired; and some reporters lose their jobs.

Earnings

Salaries for news analysts (newscasters), reporters, and correspondents vary widely but, in general, are relatively high, except at small stations and small publications where salaries are often very low. Median annual earnings of news analysts are approximately $26,470. The middle 50 percent earn between $19,210 and $40,930. The lowest 10 percent earn less than $14,100, and the highest 10 percent earn more than $70,140. Median annual earnings of news analysts in radio and television broadcasting are about $28,500.

Median annual earnings of reporters and correspondents are about $23,400. The middle 50 percent earn between $17,500 and $35,600. The lowest 10 percent earn less than $12,900, and the highest 10 percent earn more than $55,100.

Median annual earnings for writers and editors, including technical writers, are about $36,480. The middle 50 percent earn between $27,030 and $49,380 a year. The lowest 10 percent earn less than $20,920, and the highest 10 percent earn more than $76,660. Median annual earnings in the industries employing the largest numbers of writers and editors of nontechnical material are as follows:

Advertising	$38,100
Periodicals	$35,900
Books	$35,200
Newspapers	$28,500
Radio and television broadcasting	$26,300

WIRE SERVICES AND SYNDICATES

Newspapers subscribe to different wire services (United Press International and the Associated Press are the nation's leading wire services) and are able to reprint any stories that are put out over the wire. In recent years, budget cuts and staff reductions have led newspapers to rely more and more on wire service stories, thus creating a demand for more and more stringers, the position most new grads would be eligible for.

Stringers generally work on a part-time basis and are paid for each piece upon its publication. They usually cover the news in a particular geographic location and file their stories with the wire service. Stringers can also work for major newspapers who want a particular geographic area covered, but don't want to pay for a full-time writer outside the office.

Stringers with wire services can go on to become correspondents and bureau chiefs, both at home or abroad, or can use the work as a stepping-stone to full-time employment with a newspaper.

Syndicates provide features, columns, crossword puzzles, and comic strips to newspapers and magazines across the country. There are not that many slots for new writers in this business; to get your material syndicated takes an original idea that is not yet being produced, or being a name writer, such as Dave Barry or Ann Landers. A good way to start is by trying to syndicate yourself. Develop a column idea, submit a proposal and samples to various newspapers, and hope your idea gets picked up. The pay for self-syndication could be as low as $5 for each column; the idea is to sell the same article to as many different papers as possible.

MAGAZINES

Visit any bookstore or newsstand and you will see hundreds of magazines covering a variety of topics—from sports and cars to fashion and parenting. There are also many you won't see there—the hundreds of trade journals and magazines written for businesses, industries, and professional workers in as many different careers.

These publications all offer information on diverse subjects to their equally diverse readership. They are filled with articles and profiles, interviews and editorials, letters and advice, as well as pages and pages of advertisements.

Whether you work for a magazine full-time, or as an independent free-lancer, you will discover that there is no shortage of markets where you can find work or sell your articles.

Positions within magazines are very similar to those found in newspapers.

FREELANCE WRITING

A freelance writer works independently, in rented office space or in a home office. Most freelance writers plan and write articles and columns on their own, actively seeking out new markets in which to place them.

Staff writers for newspapers and magazines might have less freedom with what they choose to write, but they generally have more job security and know when their next paycheck will arrive. Freelancers trade job security and regular pay for their independence.

Both freelancers and those permanently employed have to produce high-quality work. They have editors to report to and deadlines to meet.

More and more magazines are open to working with freelancers these days. With budget cuts and staff layoffs, and because magazines don't have syndicated material to fall back on, it is generally less expensive to pay several different freelance writers by the piece, rather than employ a full-time staff writer or two.

Some freelancers are generalists; they will write about anything they think they can sell. Others are specialists, choosing to write only in a particular field, such as travel or health and medicine. Successful freelancers have a lot of market savvy; that means they are familiar with all the different publications they could market their work to, and know how to approach those publications.

Training and Qualifications

While many writers hone their writing craft in college, the business of freelancing is generally self-taught. There are, however, adult education classes throughout the country, as well as writers' associations, that can provide new freelancers with some guidance and marketing strategies.

Before starting, read as many magazines as you can, and in particular, study those you would like to write for. It's never a good idea to send an article to a magazine you have never seen before. Being familiar with the different magazines will also help you to come up with future article ideas.

Once you have decided what you want to write about, there are two ways you can proceed. You can write the entire article on spec, send it off to appropriate editors, and hope they like your topic. Or, you can write a query letter, a miniproposal, to see if there is any interest in your idea first. Query letters will save you the time of writing articles you might have difficulty selling. Only once you're given a definite assignment do you then proceed.

You can find out about different magazines and the kind of material they prefer to publish in the market guides listed at the end of this chapter.

Earnings

Getting a check for an article can be rewarding, but sadly, for new freelancers, the checks might not come often enough and are not always large enough to live on.

While staff writers are paid a regular salary (though generally not a very high one), a freelancer gets paid only when he or she sells an article. Fees could range from as low as $5 to $1,000 or more depending upon the publication. But even with a high-paying magazine, writers often have to wait until their story is published before they are paid. Because publishers work so far ahead, planning issues six months or more in advance, payment could be delayed from three months to a year or more.

To the freelancer's advantage, sometimes the same article can be sold to more than one magazine or newspaper. These resales help to increase income. You can also be paid additional money if you provide your own photographs to illustrate your articles.

Freelance writers don't need a long, impressive resume to sell their first article. The writing will speak for itself.

PUBLISHING HOUSES AND LITERARY AGENCIES

The world of publishing is a busy and exciting place, filled with risks and surprises and, sometimes, disappointments. Without the publishing world, writers would never see their words in print; there would be no magazines, newspapers, or books for the public to enjoy, no textbooks for students and teachers to work with, no written sources for information on any subject.

Those in the publishing industry wield a great deal of power. They determine which books and stories will see print, and to some extent help shape the tastes of the reading public.

It's a competitive business, with financial concerns often determining which books will get published. Editors and agents have to be able to recognize good writing and know what topics are popular and what will sell.

For editors and agents, as well as writers, there's nothing more exciting than seeing a book you worked on, whether as a writer, editor, or negotiator, finally see print and land in the bookstores. The hope is always there that the book will take off and find its way to the bestseller list and into the homes of thousands of readers. Then everyone is happy, from bookstore owners to the sales team and distributors.

But there are only ten to fifteen slots on the various bestseller lists and with thousands of books published each year, the odds are against producing a blockbuster.

Although some books have steady sales and can stay on the publishers' backlist for years, others don't do as well and can disappear from bookstore shelves after only a month or so.

Every book is a gamble; no one can ever predict what will happen. But successful editors and agents thrive on the excitement. In the publishing world, anything is possible.

Literary agents act as go-betweens for writers and editors. These days, most of the big New York publishing houses refuse to consider manuscripts unless they are sent to them by an agent. Many publishers credit agents with the ability to screen out inappropriate submissions. An agent is expected to be familiar with the different kinds of books publishers prefer to take on.

An agent spends his or her time reading manuscripts, choosing which ones to work with, and then trying to sell them to publishers. Working with an agent frees a writer to concentrate on writing instead of marketing. The agent's job is to find the right house for the client's work, and once successful, to negotiate the best financial deal for the writer. Agents also handle film rights for feature or TV movies, and foreign rights, selling books to publishers overseas.

How Publishing Houses Are Structured

A small press that puts out only three or four books a year might operate with a staff of only two or three people. Each person has to wear many hats: as acquisitions editor, finding new projects to publish; as typesetter and proofreader; as sales manager; as promoter and publicist; as clerk and secretary.

The large publishing houses, which for the most part are located in New York City, can have hundreds of employees and are separated into different departments, such as editorial, contracts, legal, sales and marketing, and publicity and promotion.

Within each department are a number of different job titles. These are some of the different positions within the editorial department, although often the duties can overlap: editorial assistant, assistant/associate editor, editor, senior editor, acquisitions editor, managing editor, production editor, executive editor, editor in chief, publisher, and president.

Editors

Editors work in book-producing publishing houses as well as for magazines and newspapers. Editors read manuscripts, talk with writers, and decide which books or stories and articles they will publish. Editors also have to read what other houses or publications are printing, to know what's out there and what's selling.

Once a manuscript is selected for publication, an editor oversees the various steps to produce the finished product, from line editing for mistakes, to the book or magazine cover art and copy. Editors also regularly attend editorial meetings and occasionally travel to writers conferences to speak to aspiring writers and to find new talent.

How Literary Agencies Are Structured

Some literary agents choose to work on their own, with little more than secretarial assistance. They can rent space in an office building or work from a home office.

Other agents prefer to work within a literary agency, either as the owner or as one of the associates. They can still function independently, choosing the writers and book projects they want to work with.

In an agency, agents must usually contribute a percentage of their income to cover the office's operating expenses.

Training and Qualifications

Most editors and agents have at least a bachelor's degree in communications, English, journalism, or any relevant liberal arts or humanities major. It is helpful to also be familiar with publishing law and contracts, and to know how to type or word process.

In publishing it's rare for someone to start out as an editor or agent without any prior experience. Many agents work for publishing houses first, becoming familiar with the editorial process and contracts before moving into a literary agency.

Within a publishing house there is a distinct ladder most editors climb as they gain experience and develop a successful track record. They usually start out as editorial assistants, answering the phone, opening and distributing the mail, and typing correspondence. Some editorial assistants are first readers for their editors, reading a manuscript then writing a reader's report. If it's a good report, the editor will take a look at the manuscript.

Most editorial assistants learn the editing process from the editor they work for and, over time, move up into editorial positions with more and more responsibility.

Earnings

Editors are generally paid a set salary. Although their salary is not dependent week to week on the sales success of the books they choose to publish, an editor with a good track record is likely to be promoted and given raises. Starting pay, however, is not particularly spectacular.

Agents, on the other hand, must sell their clients' manuscripts to publishers in order to earn any income. Agents generally work on a commission basis—10 to 15 percent of the money the writer earns. If an agent has a lot of market savvy, carefully chooses which manuscripts to represent, and has success bargaining for big advances and royalty percentages, then he or she can make a very good living, often much more than the editors to whom he or she is selling.

The downside for agents is that the marketplace is fickle, fads come and go, publishing houses merge with each other and often decrease the number of books that will see print. In a bad year, an agent might have to struggle to make a living.

RADIO AND TELEVISION STATIONS

Although the golden age of radio passed five or six decades ago, radio is still considered one of the most effective of the mass media, especially for quickly disseminating information to a large number of people. In the United States alone there are more than 10,000 radio stations on the air, with an estimated 500 million radios in use.

Television is as equally effective. Elizabeth Kolbert, writing about television in the *New York Times,* noted that: "Television has created not so much a global village as a global front stoop. Instead of gossiping about our neighbors, about whom we know less and less, we gossip about national figures, about whom we know more and more. The color set in the den has so successfully replaced the sewing circle and the hamburger joint that we are now trying to get from television that which television has caused us to give up."

Radio and television stations provide a wide range of jobs for communications majors. Several positions, such as announcers and news directors, exist in both settings and some jobs at radio stations will open otherwise closed doors at television stations.

The jobs communications majors are most qualified for are: announcer/DJ, music director, program director/production manager/public service director, news writer/editor, and scriptwriter. The duties of each job will vary depending on the format and the size of the station. Radio stations, for example, can offer specialized programming, such as country music, oldies, all-talk shows, all-news, religious broadcasts, or a combination of programming. An all-music program would require less scheduling than an all-news station. Similarly, a DJ working for a music format station will have less preparation to do than a talk show host would.

Announcer/DJ

This is the most visible and the most competitive position. Successful DJs build a rapport with their audience and can sometimes become well-known personalities. Talk-show DJs are able to articulate and defend opinions on both sides of any topic. They also need to have an entertainer's instinct for performing.

Music Director

The music director selects and organizes prerecorded music that fits the station's format. Ideally, the music director would be a fan of and knowledgeable about the station's particular area of programming, sharing the taste of the listening audience. Some music directors also double as announcers.

Program Director/Production Manager/Public Service Director

At small stations one person might handle the duties of all three job titles; at larger market stations each position will have its own director. Program directors manage a staff of announcers, writers, and producers, and schedule broadcasts on a day-to-day basis. A production manager makes sure that programs are aired on schedule, and a public service director determines which public service announcements best serve the needs of the community and deserve air time.

News Writer/Editor/Director

Personnel in the news department of radio and TV stations must keep on top of breaking news such as political events, natural disasters, and social issues. Weather and traffic reports are sometimes originated from this department as well.

News specialists must have good written and oral skills and be adept at interviewing people and conducting research.

Scriptwriter

Scriptwriters prepare copy for commercials, public service announcements, and for slots between programming. The number of openings in this area are small. The most active employers of scriptwriters are radio stations that program on air dramas and talk shows.

MULTIMEDIA

Multimedia is a catchall phrase that has come to mean a number of different things. It can be a multi-image show; a sound-enhanced slide presentation; an interactive CD-ROM program with graphics and text; or the creative use of charts, graphs, video, and photography.

Multimedia career opportunities are prevalent in the corporate world, in business and industry, in health science, in government, as well as with religious organizations, independent media production companies, and advertising agencies and PR firms.

Multimedia is used at trade shows, in boardrooms, and classrooms and to impress stockholders and attract clients and customers. The jobs in this field that are of interest to communications majors include: AV (audiovisual) producer; AV writer; production assistant; AV manager/director.

The duties of these positions all revolve around the different phases of designing, researching, writing, producing, programming, scheduling, budgeting, and distributing multimedia presentations. All these jobs require similar backgrounds and training. A bachelor's degree, specifically in mass communications, is a must, although related degrees in English or journalism will be considered. In addition to having good writing and organizational skills, some technical expertise in the use of equipment or photography is a plus.

RELATED OCCUPATIONS

Communications majors acquire skills that can be transferred to a number of related occupations. Here is a representative list of the job titles in a few similar career paths; no doubt further investigation will reveal more.

Actor	Feature film producer
Comedian	Ghostwriter
Documentary maker	Lyricist
Drama/music teacher	Musician
Educational film/video maker	Performing artist
Entertainer	Playwright
Feature film director	Poet
Feature filmmaker	Visual artist

STRATEGIES FOR FINDING JOBS

Get a Foot in the Door

In the world of newspapers, magazines, and book publishing, some experts advise that you should take any job you can to get your foot in the door. If you want to be an editor, for example, you could start out as a contract assistant, then move into an editorial position, and up the ladder to senior editor or higher. If you get yourself in the door, and get to know the people in the department for which you prefer to work, your chances are better than those of an unknown candidate who wants to go immediately into an editorial position.

The same holds true for radio and television stations. Production assistants with a proven track record, for example, will move into higher level positions than job candidates off the street.

Prepare a Portfolio/Audition Tape

For photojournalists, there are a few different routes to take in the job hunting process, but they all include putting together a professional portfolio.

Some photojournalists identify the papers they would like to work for and, at their own expense, fly out to talk to the different editors—even when they know there are currently no openings. This approach, though a bit costly for someone just starting out, can often work. The job applicant makes himself known, and when an opening does occur, potential employers will remember your top-quality portfolio.

Job hunting through the mail can be just as effective. Send out your portfolio with a good cover letter. Don't be afraid to mention any story ideas you might have. Newspapers aren't looking for robots, and they appreciate a photojournalist who does more than stand behind the camera and click the shutter.

Then follow up a week or so later as a reminder. You can make up your own picture postcards, using your best work. This helps to jog the editor's memory—and shows how creative you are.

Potential DJs and announcers, once they have a foot in the door, should be prepared to take any air time slot they are offered, even if it's six o'clock on a Sunday morning. This will give you the opportunity to tape yourself. You can constantly update your tape and use it for auditions for more critical time slots.

Internships

Another successful method is to take more than the one required college internship. If you can get involved in two or even three internships, you'll make more contacts and have a better chance of lining up full-time employment when you graduate. At the same time you'll be adding to your portfolio and creating impressive specifics to include on your resume.

HELP IN LOCATING THESE EMPLOYERS

The following listings, directories, magazines, and resource books can help you in your job search. Most are available in the reference section of your library.

Broadcasting and Cable Marketplace
R.R. Bowker
121 Chanlon Rd.
New Providence, NJ 07974
www.bowker.com

Broadcasting Yearbook
Contains a listing of television stations. (Contact information same as above.)

Encyclopedia of Associations
Gale Research, Inc.
P.O. Box 33477
Detroit, MI 48232-5477

Gale Directory of Publications and Broadcast Media
Gale Research, Inc.
P.O. Box 33477
Detroit, MI 48232-5477

Guide to Literary Agents & Art/Photo Reps
Photographer's Market
Writer's Market
Writer's Digest Books
F & W Publications
1507 Dana Ave.
Cincinnati, OH 45207

The Literary Marketplace
R.R. Bowker
121 Chanlon Rd.
New Providence, NJ 07974

National Directory of Weekly Newspapers
National Newspaper Association
1627 K St. NW, Ste. 400
Washington, DC 20006

National Public Radio
2025 M St. NW
Washington, DC 20036

Newspapers Career Directories
Gale Research, Inc.
P.O. Box 33477
Detroit, MI 48232-5477

Publishers Weekly
P.O. Box 1979
Marion, OH 43306

Writer's Digest Magazine
Writer's Digest Books
1507 Dana Ave.
Cincinnati, OH 45207
www.writersdigest.com

PROFESSIONAL ASSOCIATIONS

Deciding in what area of the media you would like to work and contacting a few of the related professional associations will help with your job search as well as your professional development. Professional associations offer conferences, seminars and workshops, a variety of publications, and job placement services.

The Accrediting Council on Education in Journalism and Mass Communications
University of Kansas School of Journalism
Stauffer-Flint Hall
Lawrence, KS 66045
www.ukans.edu/~acejmc
Services: For a list of schools with accredited programs in journalism send a stamped, self-addressed envelope.

American Society of Journalists and Authors (ASJA)
1501 Broadway, Ste. 302
New York, NY 10036
www.asja.org
Services: publications, market search, conferences, information on contract negotiations, copyright, intellectual property, and similar issues

American Society of Magazine Editors
919 Third Ave.
New York, NY 10022
Services: career information, conferences

American Society of Media Photographers
150 N. Second St.
Philadelphia, PA 19106
www.asmp.org
Services: educational programs and seminars, publications

American Society of Newspaper Editors
P.O. Box 4090
Reston, VA 22090-1700
www.asne.org
Services: convention, publications, grants for school newspapers

Association for International Broadcasting
P.O. Box 4440
Walton CO14 8BX
United Kingdom
www.aibcast.demon.co.uk/index.html
Services: publications

Association of American Publishers
71 Fifth Ave.
New York, NY 10010
www.publishers.org
Services: seminars and workshops, book fairs, publications

Association of Authors' Representatives (AAR)
P.O. Box 237201
Ansonia Station
New York, NY 10003
www.publishersweekly.com/aar
Services: publications, including Canon of Ethics, and agent membership
directory

Association of Independent TV Stations
1320 19th St. NW, Ste. 300
Washington, DC 20015
Services: publications

Association of Independent Video & Filmmakers
(also the Foundation for Independent Video and Film)
304 Hudson St., 6th Fl.

New York, NY 10013
www.aivf.org/index_basic.html
Services: training seminars, journals, resources guides, work referrals

Author's League of America
330 W. 42nd St., 29th Fl.
New York, NY 10036
Services: publications

Broadcast Education Association
1771 N St. NW
Washington, DC 20036
www.beaweb.org
Services: training, educational materials, annual convention, publications,
job placement

Canadian Magazine Publishers Association
130 Spadina Ave., Ste. 202
Toronto, ON M5V 2L4
Canada
www.cmpa.ca
Services: training, publications

The Dow Jones Newspaper Fund, Inc.
P.O. Box 300
Princeton, NJ 08543-0300
www.dowjones.com
Services: Information on careers in journalism, colleges and universities
offering degree programs in journalism or communications, and journalism
scholarships and internships

Education Writers Association
1331 H St. NW, #307
Washington, DC 20005
www.ewa.org
Services: publications, job bank, seminars, fellowships, contests

Magazine Publishers Association
919 Third Ave., 22nd Fl.
New York, NY 10022
Services: annual conference, seminars, publications

National Academy of Television Arts and Sciences
111 W. 57th St., Ste. 1050
New York, NY 10019
www.emmyonline.org
Services: workshops, seminars, publications, awards, job bank

National Association of Broadcast Employees and Technicians Communications Workers of America (NABET/CWA), International
501 Third St. NW
Washington, DC 20001
http://union.nabetcwa.org/nabet
Services: career information

National Association of Broadcasters, Career Center
1771 N St. NW
Washington, DC 20036
www.nab.org
Services: publications, career information

National Association of Broadcasters, Research and Planning Department
1771 N St. NW
Washington, DC 20036
www.nab.org
Services: employment and salary information

National Association of Independent Publishers Representatives
111 E. 14th St.
New York, NY 10003
www.naipr.org
Services: publications, conferences, job listings

National Cable Television Association
1724 Massachusetts Ave. NW
Washington, DC 20036
www.ncta.com
Services: publications, career information

National Newspaper Association
1525 Wilson Blvd., Ste. 550
Arlington, VA 22209

Services: Publications, career information, including a pamphlet titled *Newspaper Careers and Challenges for the Next Century*

National Press Photographers Association (NPPA)
3200 Cloasdaile Dr., Ste. 306
Durham, NC 27705
www.nppa.org
Services: annual television-newsfilm workshop, publications, job bank, membership directory

Newsletter & Electronic Publishers Association
1501 Wilson Blvd., Ste. 509
Arlington, VA 22209
www.newsletters.org
Services: publications, conferences, professional development

The Newspaper Guild
Research and Information Department
501 3rd St. NW, Ste. 250
Washington, DC 20001
www.newsguild.org
Services: Information on union wage rates for newspaper and magazine reporters

Newspaper Association of America
1921 Gallows Rd., Ste. 600
Vienna, VA 22182
www.naa.org
Services: publications, including pamphlets titled *Newspaper Career Guide* and *Newspaper: What's In It for Me?*

Radio and Television News Directors Foundation
1000 Connecticut Ave. NW
Washington, DC 20036
www.rtndf.org
Services: publications, career information, job placement, scholarships, internships

Society of National Association Publications
1150 Connecticut Ave. NW, Ste. 1050
Washington, DC 20036

www.snaponline.org
Services: seminars and resource networks, publications, job listings

Society for Technical Communication, Inc.
901 N. Stuart St., Ste. 904
Arlington, VA 22203
www.stc.org
Services: career information

Writers Guild of America (East)
555 W. 57th St., Ste. 1230
New York, NY 10019
www.wgaeast.org
Services: resources for writers, seminars, script registration

Writers Guild of America (West)
7000 W. Third St.
Los Angeles, CA 90048
www.wga.org

CHAPTER THIRTEEN

PATH 4: COMMUNICATION DISORDERS

While many communications majors devote their professional careers to ensuring effective communication within corporations, with the media, with consumers, or through human and social service programs, there are those who prefer to work with individuals who suffer from a wide range of communication disorders.

These practitioners, who are commonly called speech-language pathologists or audiologists, are communicators as effective as the professionals whose jobs we explored in earlier chapters, but they have a different focus, work with a different public, and have a different set of acquired skills.

According to the American Speech-Language-Hearing Association (ASHA), speech and language disorders are "inabilities of individuals to understand and/or appropriately use the speech and language systems of society. Such disorders may range from simple sound repetitions or occasional miscalculations to the complete absence of the ability to use speech and language for communication."

For every twenty Americans who communicate "normally," there is one individual who is afflicted with a speech-language disorder. They number nearly ten million people.

Hearing impairment ranges from the inability to hear speech and other sounds loudly enough or understand speech even when it is loud enough, to the complete loss of all hearing.

Based on studies conducted a decade ago by the National Center for Health Statistics, it is estimated that hearing impairment in one or both ears affects approximately two out of every one hundred school-age children; twenty-nine out of every one hundred people sixty-five years of age or older; and a total of 21.2 million Americans.

A career as a speech-language pathologist or audiologist offers an opportunity to help and interact with a wide variety of individuals, providing rewarding experiences for both the client and therapist. It is also a career suited for the researcher dedicated to finding new therapeutic approaches and technology.

DEFINITION OF THE CAREER PATH

Speech-Language Pathology

A speech-language pathologist has a wide range of duties and choice of settings, age groups, and disorders to work with. Speech-language pathologists screen, evaluate, and treat people with communication disorders. They also make referrals, provide counseling and instruction, supervise students and clinical fellows, teach, conduct research, and administer speech-language pathology programs.

Speech and language disorders can include:

Disfluencies including stuttering and other interruptions of normal speech flow, such as excessive hesitations, repeating the first sound in a word over and over, or too frequently inserting extraneous syllables ("er" or "um") or words and phrases into speech

Articulation disorders, substituting one sound for another ("free" instead of "three"), omitting a sound, or distorting a sound

Voice disorders, inappropriate pitch, quality, loudness, resonance, and duration

Aphasia or complete loss of speech (generally resulting from a stroke or head injury)

Delayed language ability

Those working in elementary schools spend a great deal of the time providing articulation therapy or phonologic therapy, teaching children to articulate more clearly. Some of the techniques they use involve playing games that have the child work with the same target sounds. Another technique is called auditory bombardment. It uses a set of headphones that amplifies the therapist's speech and plays it into the child's ear. The therapist reads a list of words that are amplified, helping the child focus on the correct sounds.

Another exciting and unfortunately common disorder for speech-language pathologists to deal with is aphasia, an inability to either understand or produce speech due to a brain injury or brain disorder. This condition is most commonly the result of a stroke and sometimes the consequence of brain trauma or an accident.

Although speech-language pathologists rely less heavily on devices than audiologists, they do use equipment to check the health of vocal cords and detect any abnormal growths.

Audiology

The primary functions of audiologists are testing hearing and doing rehabilitation work with hearing-impaired individuals and their significant others.

To test hearing and the functioning of the auditory system, audiologists use a range of electronic equipment, the audiometer, and other devices for assessing performance of hearing aids. These include devices that plug into hearing aids and can be programmed so that the performance of the hearing aid is appropriate for the hearing loss of that individual. There are also devices that employ very tiny microphones that are hooked up into tubes inserted directly into the ear canal to tell just how much sound is reaching the ear drum. Other devices test the functioning of a hearing aid independently of a person, ensuring that all the electronics in the aid are working correctly.

Hearing loss affects a person's ability to communicate and the ability to hear speech. For most people, the most important person they want to be able to communicate with is their spouse or significant other. Therefore, therapy will focus not only on the hearing-impaired individual but on the spouse as well. Emphasis is placed on teaching good communication skills—everything from learning not to start a conversation from another room, to getting rid of other sources of noise by turning off the dishwasher or TV.

Audiologists use other techniques to help improve communication. They teach hearing individuals who want to be understood by hearing- impaired individuals to announce the topic they want to discuss before launching into it or to announce topic changes before making the change.

If the hearing-impaired person has a hard time understanding, he or she can say "I understood we're talking about such and such, or you said something about the dog, but I didn't catch it all." This gives the other person feedback, telling them what has been understood, rather than simply saying "What?" The significant other of the hearing-impaired person can learn to rephrase what he or she has said, instead of just repeating the same sentence the person had trouble with in the first place.

In cases with more profound hearing loss, audiologists spend their time working on teaching the person to use what little hearing he or she has as well as working with other systems to help with speech and how to get along without hearing. Audiologists work with lip-reading skills, sign language, and some simple devices such as a light in place of the doorbell, telephone, or alarm clock tones. The audiologist would be knowledgeable of these devices and able to make them available to clients.

Teaching

The old saying that "those who can, do, those who can't, teach" doesn't apply here. In order for someone to become an instructor or professor in a university's communication disorders program, he or she must first become a certified speech-language pathologist or audiologist and fulfill all the requisite hours for practicing in the field. Those who return to the classroom after a stint in practice bring with them a wealth of hands-on experience in addition to their theoretical knowledge.

A Ph.D. is the usual requirement for entry into university teaching in a communications disorders program, as well as demonstrating an interest in guiding and supervising student therapists.

With such a nationwide shortage of certified speech-language pathologists and audiologists, the demand is on the increase for more teachers who can, in turn, turn out more qualified personnel.

Research

There are those who, rather than practice or teach, are more interested in a career in research. They are fascinated by the different problems human communication presents and work to find solutions to prevent, identify, assess, or rehabilitate speech, language, or hearing disorders.

ASHA reports the following advances that research scientists have made. They now know that:

Communication starts long before babies say their first words.

Hearing can be measured at super-high frequency levels.

Every individual has a unique voice that can be used for identification, much the same way fingerprints are used.

Damage to different areas in the brain results in different types of language problems.

Technology can be used to develop better hearing aids, electronic voice boxes, and computers for communication.

In addition to sensing sound, the ear is also capable of producing sound (cochlear emissions).

Areas of interest for researchers include:

Investigating the physical, biological, and physiological factors underlying normal communication

Exploring the impact of social, psychological, and psychophysiological factors on communication disorders

Cooperating with other professionals, such as engineers, physicians, and educators, to develop a comprehensive approach to working with people with communication disorders

Researchers are most often affiliated with universities, dividing their time between classroom teaching and work on various research questions. The usual requirement for a research scientist is a minimum of a Ph.D. degree.

Some research scientists work in industrial settings, for pharmaceutical companies, or for manufacturers of hearing aids or computers.

POSSIBLE JOB TITLES

Professionals in the field are given a variety of job titles including speech clinician, speech pathologist, speech therapist, speech teacher, and speech correctionist. The job title preferred by ASHA is speech-language pathologist. Audiologists are sometimes referred to as hearing therapists or hearing teachers. Another general job title could be communication or communicative disorders specialist.

Within an educational setting, speech-language pathologists fall under the institution's ranking system and have titles such as full, associate, or assistant professor. Communication science researchers or research scientists are also based at universities.

POSSIBLE EMPLOYERS

Medical Clinics

Therapists working in a medical clinic setting come into contact with many different people who have a wide variety of disorders. They are able to establish close relationships with their clients because they work with them over a period of time. The relationship usually begins from the point before they've had the cause of the disorder diagnosed, through the diagnosis, and treatment and therapy.

Therapists in this setting also get to work closely with other professionals—physicians, nurses, neurology professionals, psychologists, physical therapists—to collaborate on effective treatment plans.

Hospitals

Therapists who work in outpatient hospital departments function similarly to those in outpatient medical clinics. They also work with inpatients who are recovering from strokes, head injuries, or other problems affecting communication that would require hospitalization.

Nursing Homes/Rehab Centers

In these settings, therapists work with elderly patients or patients who have recovered enough from their stroke or injury to be released from the hospital but are not yet independent enough to return home. Work duties consist mainly of diagnosing and carrying out treatment plans.

Public Schools

Here, the speech-language pathologist works with children, most commonly treating them in a group situation. Children with similar problems would be excused from their regular classrooms for an hour, two or three times a week, to work on particular speech disorders.

Some speech-language pathologists are based at one school, while others travel to several different schools within the district.

In a school setting, screening for hearing impairment is usually done by the school nurse. The audiologist works more with diagnosis and therapy.

Private Schools

The situation in private schools for speech-language pathologists and audiologists is similar to work in the public schools.

State Schools for the Deaf and Similar Institutions

Therapists at these institutions work with a more narrow range of problems. Students might all be deaf, or perhaps deaf and blind. Students and therapists would meet on a more regular basis than in public or private school settings, and the work would focus mainly on improving speech skills.

Working with completely deaf or deaf and blind children is by far the most challenging—and for some the most rewarding—area of the communication disorders field.

Private Practice

Speech-language pathologists and audiologists can carve out an excellent career for themselves in private practice. Their services are covered by insurance and they can visit clients in their homes or set up their own offices and take referrals from hospitals; ear, nose, and throat (ENT) specialists; and other professionals in the medical community.

Because the schools don't have enough staff to serve all the students who have been identified as having communication disorders, private practitioners also receive referrals through the school board. During the summer months, when schools are closed, parents might take their child to a private practice speech-language pathologist to continue the therapy started during the regular school year.

Home Health Care Agencies

Home health care agencies operate on both local and national levels. A therapist or audiologist registered with a local agency will be given assignments as requests come in. National agencies are used by hospitals and other concerns all over the country and provide an opportunity for a practitioner to travel to different cities on short- or long-term assignments.

Colleges and Universities

Some experienced speech-language pathologists and audiologists choose to work in an academic setting, teaching students preparing for careers in communication disorders.

The typical college or university instructor has spent four years beyond the master's degree, earning a Ph.D. In addition, the majority have master's degrees in speech pathology and have worked in the field before returning to the classroom as instructors.

The Ph.D. degree is primarily a research degree, preparing the recipient to do research in speech or hearing disorders.

The job prospects are good at this level because there are fewer people choosing teaching over practicing in the field. In fact, it is not unheard of for some professors to leave their teaching post and return to field work. The salaries are better in the field, but universities offer longer vacations and sometimes lighter workloads. For those more interested in teaching and research than actual practice, the academic setting is ideal.

WORKING CONDITIONS

The work you do will depend on the type of clientele your hiring institution serves. The range of settings we've just covered suggests there is a wide variety of people to be served by this profession.

Your hours will also depend on the setting. If your duties consist of mainly diagnostic work or testing, you would see a larger number of clients per week than if you were doing more therapy.

In schools, you might work the same number of hours as classroom teachers—or less. Most of your time would be spent in testing, screening, diagnosing, providing therapy, and supervising noncertified B.A.-level speech-language pathologists or master's-level pathologists fulfilling the requirements for their clinical fellowship year.

Those working in medical settings generally avoid the shift work that most nurses and other medical personnel are subject to.

Speech-language pathologists and audiologists working at a university teaching future pathologists, generally divide their workload evenly among these three activities: teaching, research, and supervising graduate students. In addition, university professors are responsible for other duties associated with academic life, including administering and grading exams, classroom preparation, attending departmental meetings, and maintaining regular office hours.

TRAINING AND QUALIFICATIONS

Just as with other communications programs, programs in speech-language pathology and audiology can be housed in a number of different university departments with a number of different names and degrees conferred. Commonly, programs are called communication disorders, communicative disorders, communication science, speech communications, speech pathology, and speech-language and hearing pathology. The program name preferred by ASHA is communication sciences and disorders. Degrees conferred could be a Master of Science, Master of Arts, or Master of Education.

The American Speech-Language-Hearing Association certifies speech-language pathologists and audiologists who have met certain criteria. To become certified and awarded a certificate of clinical competence in speech-language pathology (CCC-SLP) or a certificate of clinical competence in audiology (CCC-A), or certificates in both areas, candidates must:

Earn a master's degree covering the requisite number of credit hours from an institution whose program is accredited by the Educational Standard Board of the American Speech-Language-Hearing Association.

Complete the requisite number of hours in a supervised clinical observation and a supervised clinical practicum. The practicum cannot be undertaken until sufficient coursework for such an experience has been completed.

Complete a clinical fellowship of at least thirty-six weeks of full-time professional experience or its part-time equivalent in a variety of settings.

The master's degree in speech pathology and audiology entails at least 350 hours of clinical contact with patients or clients with communication disorders.

Following the master's program, the final step towards certification is the successful completion of a clinical fellowship year. Often, the first nine months of your job working full-time can be considered as your clinical fellowship year. During that time, you would have a certified speech-language pathologist supervising your work. If you were working only half-time, it would take you longer to complete the clinical fellowship year.

The clinical fellowship gives you a chance to integrate all you have learned through coursework and the clinical practicum.

Bachelor's-degree programs are available in communication disorders, and many have coursework designed to mesh with a master's program. However, a B.A. in speech-language pathology or communication disorders is not required to enter a master's program in speech-language pathology.

Because of the shortage of certified communication disorders specialists, some bachelor's-level pathologists do find work. But, the only setting in which they can be employed with just a bachelor's degree is within different public school systems in some states. And they must sign a contract promising to get their master's within four to seven years.

They are allowed to work toward the master's while they are employed, but that can be problematic. Most people working within the public schools are on duty during the times that graduate courses are offered. Some night courses are available, but in some states, the programs are not currently designed to accommodate the schedule of working students.

In addition to the coursework, you need between 350 and 375 contact hours in a practicumn experience, some of which must be acquired in several different settings working with different types of disorders and different age groups. If you are in the public schools, the logistics become very difficult.

Some employed B.A.-level pathologists take a sabbatical from their job in order to finish. Most find going straight for the master's degree without working to be the most efficient method.

ASHA publishes a handbook that specifies the exact requirements for professional certification. You can contact them at the address listed at the end of this chapter.

Currently, there are thirty-nine states that legally require individuals who engage in private practice or who work in non-public agencies to hold a license in speech-language pathology or audiology. Generally, the requirements are similar to those for ASHA certification. ASHA also maintains a list of all state licensing boards and of all accredited university programs in speech-language pathology and audiology.

CAREER OUTLOOK

Projections indicate that job openings will strip the supply of qualified candidates for the next ten years.

The following state departments of education reported experiencing critical shortages of speech-language pathologists and audiologists:

Alabama	Nebraska
Alaska	Nevada
Arizona	New Mexico
Delaware	New York
Florida	North Carolina
Idaho	North Dakota
Indiana	Oklahoma
Kentucky	South Carolina
Louisiana	South Dakota
Mississippi	Wyoming
Montana	

Other states are also experiencing shortages, but at a lower percentage rate.

The American Hospital Association (AHA) reports chronic shortages in key hospital occupations, including speech-language pathologists. In 1991 one out of every ten speech-language pathologist position remained unfilled, a vacancy percentage that continues today.

The increased demand for speech-language pathologists and audiologists has multiple causes, one of which is related to the new insurance coverage for home health care. There are now companies that operate franchises in different parts of the country, hiring paramedical professionals—speech pathologists, audiologists, nurses, physical therapists—to provide health services to people in their homes. With the increase in insurance coverage there has been an increased market for those types of professionals.

Legislative recognition of the need for certified speech-language pathologists and audiologists in the public schools has also contributed to the shortage. The Individuals with Disability Education Act and the Americans with Disabilities Act, as well as others, prohibit employers and educational institutions from discriminating on the basis of handicap and to provide necessary and reasonable accommodations. In addition to wheelchair ramps that everyone is now familiar with, this also takes into account other considerations, such as decreasing noise levels in the area where a hearing-impaired person is working.

The laws also mandate that the personnel who provide services to children must be adequately and appropriately prepared in the area in which they provide these services. As school districts strive to comply with the law they will be hiring more and more speech, language, and hearing professionals.

The following list includes other indicators of increasing employment opportunities in this career path:

Higher success rate at saving children at birth with potential for communication disorders

A substantial increase in referrals of preschool and schoolage children for speech-language and hearing services

More emphasis on preventative health measures

Larger bilingual populations. Estimates suggest that more than five million individuals from diverse backgrounds have a speech, language, or hearing disability.

National public health policy plans for early identification and diagnosis of hearing disorders in infants and toddlers

Ongoing promotional efforts by ASHA and other concerned associations to raise public awareness

This is good news for future speech-language pathologists and audiologists. Not only are there plum jobs waiting for you upon graduation, but money is now available to see you through training. In an attempt to meet the need for more trained professionals, scholarship programs have been set up throughout the country on local and state levels as well as through individual university graduate programs. Some of these programs guarantee employment upon graduation.

To find out more about the various scholarships that are available, check with ASHA, local school boards, or through graduate communication disorders programs at universities.

In summary, job prospects across the country are excellent and will continue to be for some time.

EARNINGS

According to a recent survey conducted by the American Speech-Language-Hearing Association, the median annual salary for full-time certified speech-language pathologists or audiologists who work eleven or twelve months annually is $44,000. For those who work nine or ten months annually, median annual salaries for speech-language pathologists are $40,000; for audiologists, $42,000.

Median annual earnings in the industries employing the largest number of speech-language pathologists and audiologists are as follows:

Hospitals	$44,800
Offices of other health care practitioners	$44,500
Elementary and secondary schools	$38,400

STRATEGIES FOR FINDING THE JOBS

This is one career path where communication disorders majors won't need much help locating a job. Because of the shortage of certified audiologists and speech-language pathologists, graduates will find they have their choice of geographic location and job setting. However, to make sure you don't miss out hearing about any of the best slots, there are some avenues you can pursue to keep yourself informed.

The American Speech-Language-Hearing Association maintains a computerized placement service and job openings are regularly announced in the professional journals.

Many university departments also hold career days and job fairs, inviting employers from around the country to meet with students and conduct mini-interviews right on the spot.

If you already have preferences for settings or geographic location, you can call the individual personnel departments and let them know of your interest.

PROFESSIONAL ASSOCIATIONS

ASHA is the main professional association for speech-language pathologists and audiologists. It has more than 99,000 members and certificate holders and recognizes fifty state speech and hearing association affiliates. It provides certification to qualified speech-language pathologists and audiologists and accreditation to qualifying university programs.

Academy of Dispensing Audiologists
1407 York Rd., Ste. 201
Lutherville, MD 21093

Academy of Neurologic Communication Disorders and Sciences
Vanderbilt Bill Wilkerson Center
1114 19th Ave. S.
Nashville, TN 37212

Academy of Rehabilitative Audiology
University of Florida
4419 NW 22nd St.
Gainesville, FL 32605

Air Force Audiology Association
11631 Rousseau
San Antonio, TX 78251

American Academy of Audiology
8201 Greensboro Dr., Ste. 300
McLean, VA 22102

**American Academy of Private Practice in Speech-Language Pathology
and Audiology**
4341 S. Westnedge, Ste. 2104
Kalamazoo, MI 49008

American Auditory Society
512 E. Canterbury Ln.
Phoenix, AZ 85022

American Speech-Language-Hearing Association (ASHA)
10801 Rockville Pike
Rockville, MD 20852
http://professional.asha.org/contents.htm
Members/Purpose: Speech-language pathologists and audiologists.
Training: Clinical certification board; educational programs/workshops.
Journal/Publication: *ASHA; American Journal of Audiology; American
Journal of Speech-Language Pathology; Journal of Speech and Hearing
Research; Language, Speech, and Hearing Services in Schools; Guide to
Graduate Education in Speech-Language Pathology and Audiology;* brochures
and videos on careers.
Job Listings: Professional referrals; placement service.

Asian Pacific Islander Caucus
San Diego State University
Dean's Office, Hepner Hall 124 CHHs
San Diego, CA 92182

Audiology Foundation of America
207 North St.
West Lafayette, IN 47906

Communication Disorders Prevention and Epidemiology Study Group
200 Anderson Rd.
King of Prussia, PA 19406

Council for Accreditation in Occupational Hearing Conservation
611 E. Wells St.
Milwaukee, WI 53202
www.caohc.org

Council of Audiology Programs
Central Michigan University
1339 Tomah Dr.
Mt. Pleasant, MI 48858

Council of Graduate Programs in Communication Sciences and Disorders
University of Kansas at Lawrence
Department of Speech, Language, Hearing and Sciences
University of Kansas, Dole Bldg.
Lawrence, KS 66045

Council of Language, Speech and Hearing Consultants in State Education Agencies
West Virginia Department of Education
Bldg. 6, Rm. 304
1900 Kanawha Blvd.
Charleston, WV 25305

Council of School Supervisors
619 Academy Ave.
Matteson, IL 60443

Council of State Association Presidents
1382 Fourth Ave. NE
Sioux Center, IA 51250

Council of Supervisors in Speech-Language Pathology and Audiology
1605 Gage Dr.
Middletown, OH 45042

Directors of Speech and Hearing Programs in State Health and Welfare Agencies
Audiology and Speech-Language Consultants
Children's Special Health Care Services
Michigan Department of Public Health
P.O. Box 30195, Rm. 217
Lansing, MI 48909

Educational Audiology Association
18160 Gages Lake Rd.
Gages Lake, IL 60030

Hispanic Caucus
167 Park Pl.
Brooklyn, NY 11238

Human Communication Coalition
3707 7th St., NW
Rochester, MN 55901

Infant and Family Special Interest Group
Frank Porter Graham Child Development Center
CB 8185
University of North Carolina at Chapel Hill
Chapel Hill, NC 27599

International Affairs Association
1808 Princeton NE
Albuquerque, NM 87106

International Association of Orofacial Myology
P.O. Box 6503
Bellevue, WA 98008

Lesbian, Gay, and Bisexual Audiologists and Speech-Language Pathologists
329 10th St. NE
Washington, DC 20002

Military Audiology Association
P.O. Box 30483
Alexandria, VA 22310-8483
www.militaryaudiology.org

National Academy of Pre-Professional Programs in Communication Sciences and Disorders
2785 Veach Rd.
Owensboro, KY 42303

National Black Association for Speech, Language, and Hearing
P.O. Box 50605
Washington, DC 20091-0605

National Council of State Boards of Examiners for Speech-Language Pathology and Audiology
925 Yankee St.
Wellsburg, WV 26070

National Cued Speech Association
Nazareth College
4245 East Ave.
Rochester, NY 14618

National Hearing Conservation Association
9101 E. Kenyon Ave., Ste. 3000
Denver, CO 80237-1855

Native American Caucus
4212 N. 16th St.
Phoenix, AZ 85016

Navy Audiology Society
Occupational Audiology Department
Naval Medical Center Portsmouth
Lafayette River Annex

6500 Hampton Blvd.
Norfolk, VA 23508-1298

Neuro-Developmental Treatment Association
416 Yale Ave.
Alma, MI 48801

Public School Caucus
503 Forest Circle
Irving, TX 75062

**Treatment Research in Communication Disorders–
Special Interest Group**
Wilkerson Speech & Hearing Center
Vanderbilt University
1114 19th Ave. S
Nashville, TN 37232

United States Society for Augmentative and Alternative Communication
P.O. Box 5271
Evanston, IL 60204-5271

INDEX